Study Guide and Workbook

WESTERN HERITAGE BRIEF

Volume II: Since 1648

Donald Kagan
YALE UNIVERSITY

Steven Ozment
HARVARD UNIVERSITY

Frank M. Turner
YALE UNIVERSITY

Prepared by
Anthony M. Brescia
Department of History
NASSAU COMMUNITY COLLEGE

Prentice Hall
Upper Saddle River, New Jersey 07458

D1402533

© 1996 by PRENTICE-HALL, INC.
Simon and Schuster/A Viacom Company
Upper Saddle River, New Jersey 07458

10 9 8 7 6 5 4 3 2 1

ISBN 0-13-439241-8
Printed in the United States of America

VOLUME II

Chapter   *Page*

INTRODUCTION

WELCOME to the Brief edition of the *Guide*. Users of this study tool will find the sections updated and corresponding to the *Western Heritage Brief*. Note that while the "Further Consideration" sections have been preserved, those corresponding to the original documents presented in each chapter are now located at the end of every fifth chapter of the *Guide*.

Generally defined, history is learning about humankind's continuing experience by inquiry. It is the process of asking questions about things that have happened, are happening, and are likely to happen in the future. History deals with the essence of being human. It is one of the studies that most clearly separates the human species from all others. From the very beginning of human development peoples have asked, "What's happening'?" Why have they done so? What is it about us that causes the questions to be asked? It is the human species, collectively, and each of us alone that has the capacity to think and reason beyond the present. To be human is to be historical. No other creature is endowed with the ability to consider time and space, what has gone before and what will come after. To understand civilization one must also contemplate death. You and I are among the only animals of the earth who early in life must come to grips with the inevitability of our own mortality. So that we may each better understand these realities the study of history has become the structured process that is organized to reflect the growth of civilizations and the development of their human cargo.

No matter what is said about the study of history, our understanding of the past remains the core of a liberal arts education, the mark of an educated person, and an essential adjunct to our lives, regardless of career choice. This is true because many of the methods used to learn about the past are similar to the skills we use to understand the present. We are, in fact, doing little more than very carefully and thoughtfully reading the newspaper of today's past. By so doing, and by drawing on the skills of the text writers, we are seeking an enlightened, manageable, and comprehensible view of what has been.

The study of history is both a joy and a discipline. It is a joy because it brings into our lives much of the fascinating past. Yet, because there is so much of that past available to us, historical research or study can be a chore, although it need not be.

This edition of the *Guide is* designed to serve students seeking a better understanding of their own heritage within that of the West. It can be used to improve one's grade and also one's overall study skills. Any student, whatever his or her ability, will benefit from the commentary and exercises provided. The *Guide is* another means by which your instructor, the authors of the textbook, and this workbook, hope to guide you through this study of the past.

As noted below, the chapter related exercises are designed to reinforce the historical ideas and thoughts presented within each chapter of the textbook. Attention is also called to historical persons and events that are essential to understanding the fabric of the past. Virtually all chapters include map exercises. A series of questions that draw closer attention to the documents will be found after every fifth chapter of the *Guide*.

Designed as a supplement to the text, this volume can be used to gain an overall view of a particular chapter, and to call attention to selected items of historical importance within each chapter. The use of this *Guide* also provides an opportunity to test yourself on the material you have read in each chapter. These short-answer-type questions are of a kind commonly found and increasingly utilized at various levels of our educational system and in many subject areas. These questions are intended to sharpen your understanding of the chapter and to help in the comprehension of the historic data, whereas the essay questions are aimed at encouraging thought and an understanding of the larger concepts developed within each chapter. Map exercises are provided so that places and their importance in the historical picture are not lost. Continued attention has been given to physical geography in this edition. The *Guide* is arranged by chapters that correspond to those of the text. As in previous editions the page numbers corresponding to the textbook are appropriately provided throughout. Within each chapter of this Guide you will find the following:

COMMENTARY

A brief overview that highlights the development of each chapter, this section is intended to present an overall understanding of the chapter. You should read this section for a preview and later as a review of the text material.

IDENTIFICATIONS [HISTORICAL]

These are a selection of notable terms, places, events, and persons that are introduced in the chapter. *It should he noted that these identifications are only a selected sample.* They are designed to call your attention to those historical factors that are beyond the obvious and therefore appear to be of lesser importance. Use this section to deepen your understanding of specific items within each chapter.

MAP EXERCISES

These exercises, marked A and B, are intended to familiarize you with the geography and the location of important places, events, and boundaries within a specific region or wider area. Some of these exercises will require you to consult other sources or an atlas.

SHORT-ANSWER EXERCISES

The multiple-choice, true-false, and completion questions are designed to help you check on specific points and ideas developed within the chapter. These questions are not intended to be difficult, and you should be able to answer them after a reasonably careful study of the chapter. The correct answers are provided at the end of each chapter, along with the appropriate page references to *The Western Heritage Brief*.

FOR FURTHER CONSIDERATION

These essay questions are aimed at provoking thought about the wider concepts and historical problems raised within each chapter; BUT are generally different than those found at the end of each chapter of the text itself.

And grouped after every five chapters,

FOR FURTHER CONSIDERATION OF THE DOCUMENTS:

These essay questions are designed to provoke some thoughtful analysis respective to the special, boxed documents presented in the previous five chapters. Page numbers are provided as a reference back to these documents. These questions are generally different than those found in the document section of the text itself.

Paths to Constitutionalism and Absolutism: England and France in the Seventeenth Century

Commentary

The constitutional crisis in England that followed Elizabeth's reign and continued until the end of the seventeenth century had a lasting impact on Western political life. This crisis was the result of long-developing conflict between the crown and commons. This struggle cost Charles I his head, and in the end Parliament emerged the victor. Parliamentary success was due in part to the uncompromising nature of both James I and his son Charles I. Their resolute attempts to hold onto the royal prerogatives against all political and religious opposition was an ominous factor in their defeat. During the civil war of the 1640s, Charles I was not able to resolve the conflict, and his authority slipped away. As has so often occurred in modern times, a strong man with the backing of the military reinstated executive authority, though under a different title. With the death of this man—Oliver Cromwell—in 1658 the situation went full circle. Charles I's son, Charles II, ascended the bloodstained throne with Parliamentary sanction and initiated what is referred to as the Stuart Restoration. In time, however, what had appeared under Charles II as a resolution of England's troubles worsened when his brother James II confirmed the family's Catholic sympathies. Parliament quickly dispatched James II and requested his son-in-law and daughter, William of Orange [Netherlands] and Mary, to be the sovereigns of England. From a relatively docile position under Elizabeth, the House of Commons, by the time of the Glorious Revolution, had been responsible for and directly involved in the ascendancy of three English rulers: Oliver Cromwell, Charles II, and William and Mary.

By comparison this was not a period of political transition for France, at least not in the ordinary sense. Rather, by the late seventeenth century the French monarchy had achieved its goal of centuries past: absolute control of the state and the French people. This success came as a result of the self-serving reform interests of the monarchs beginning with Henry IV in 1589 and was coupled with a series of especially ruthless prime ministers. Men such as Richelieu and Mazarin wielded enormous power and left in their wake a well-ordered governmental structure ready-made for the absolutist training of Louis XIV. Louis XIV surrounded himself with capable advisers, military reformers, and financial experts. The net result was his personal control of the state exemplified by the palace complex at Versailles and France's commanding position in the European international order. The French wars of expansion in this era were meant to cap French glory but were thwarted by a combination of European states led by the Dutch United Provinces and ascendant England aligned against the threat. Political power, European hegemony, localized territorial gains, and religious attitudes were all factors in the four wars of Louis XIV. When these wars ended, France remained a great power, but a power no longer above Europe and one whose future, because of the Sun King's excesses, would soon be in doubt.

IDENTIFICATIONS

Identify each one of the following as used in the text. Refer to the text as necessary.

	Text Page
Millenary Petition	307
Duke of Buckingham	308-309
Petition of Right	308
Short Parliament	310
Grand Remonstrance	310
Cavaliers and Roundheads	311
"Pride's Purge"	312
Clarendon Code	313
English Bill of Rights of 1689	314
"one king, one law, one faith"	315
intendants	316
Fronde	317
Bishop Bossuet	319
Cornelius Jansen	321
mercantilism	321
Sebastien Vauban	322
Prince of Orange	323-325
Battle of Malplaquet	327
Peace of Utrecht-Rastadt	327

MAP EXERCISE A

3

CHAPTER 13
PATHS TO
CONSTITUTIONALISM AND
ABSOLUTISM: ENGLAND
AND FRANCE IN THE
SEVENTEENTH CENTURY

Locate each of the following areas on the accompanying map:

1. Irish Sea
2. English Channel
3. North Sea
4. Thames River
5. River Seine
6. Aix-la-Chapelle
7. Plymouth
8. Paris
9. Versailles
10. Nantes
11. Brussels
12. Utrecht
13. Amsterdam
14. Marston Moor
15. Naseby
16. Cambridge
17. London
18. Wales

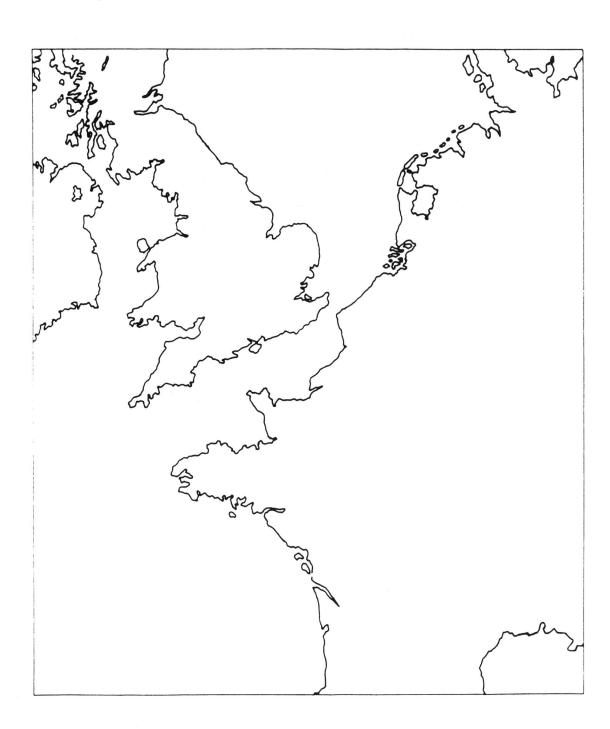

MAP EXERCISE B

On this map of France, locate and mark each of the following areas and cities:

RIVERS:	Garonne, Loire, Rhone, Seine
MOUNTAINS:	Central Massif, Pyrenees, Vosges
WATERS:	Bay of Biscay, English Channel, Pas de Calais
CITIES:	Bordeaux, Cherbourg, La Rochelle, Le Havre, Lyons, Marseilles, Metz, Nancy, Nantes, Paris, Strasbourg, Tours, Versailles

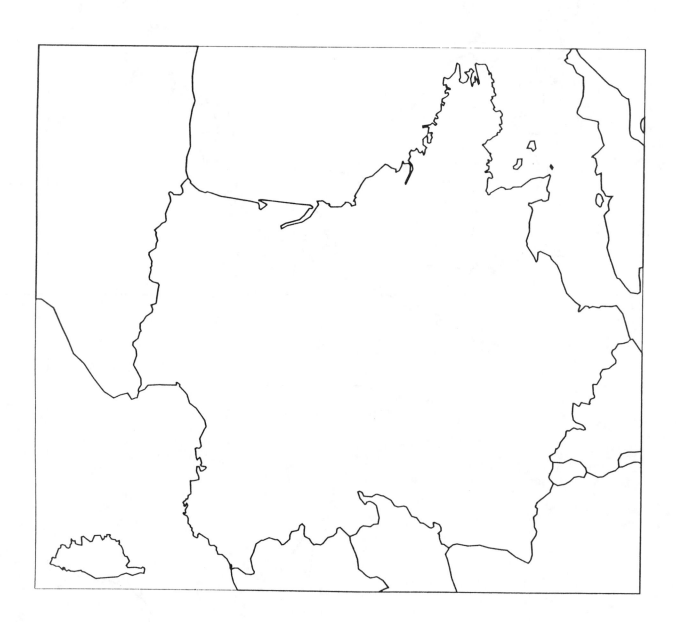

SHORT-ANSWER EXERCISES

5

CHAPTER 13
PATHS TO
CONSTITUTIONALISM AND
ABSOLUTISM: ENGLAND
AND FRANCE IN THE
SEVENTEENTH CENTURY

Multiple-Choice

_____ 1. The book *A Trew Law of Free Monarchies* was written by: (a) James VI of Scotland, (b) John Locke, (c) Charles I, (d) Oliver Cromwell.

_____ 2. Early religious differences between James I and the Puritans fostered the founding of: (a) Puritannia, (b) Massachusetts Bay Colony, (c) Maryland, (d) New Amsterdam (New York).

_____ 3. Which of the following was least supportive of English monarchial government in the period 1620 through the 1640s: (a) Duke of Buckingham, (b) John Pym, (c) Thomas Wentworth, (d) William Laud.

_____ 4. The so-called Test Act was largely aimed at discrediting: (a) Titus Oates, (b) James, duke of York, (c) Charles II, (d) earl of Shaftsbury.

_____ 5. The reason for the continuing opposition to the reign of James II was his: (a) imprisonment of Anglican bishops, (b) appointments of known Catholics to high offices, (c) insistence upon the repeal of the Test Act, (d) all of these.

_____ 6. Which of the following was least directly responsible for the establishment of absolutism in France during the seventeenth century: (a) Louis XIII, (b) Sully, (c) Richelieu, (d) Mazarin.

_____ 7. Jansenists believed that: (a) human beings had been redeemed through Christ's death, (b) Cornelis Jansen should be canonized, (c) that human beings could not be redeemed without special grace from God, (d) St. Augustine had incorrectly interpreted the concept of original sin.

_____ 8. The marquis of Louvois is noted for all of the following except: (a) establishing a professional French army, (b) developing a system of trench warfare, (c) introducing a merit-based system of promotion, (d) increasing army pay.

_____ 9. Louis XIV considered the revocation of the Edict of Nantes as: (a) unimportant, (b) militarily significant, (c) his most pious act, (d) good for business.

_____ 10. The correct chronological order of these important treaties negotiated during the wars of Louis XIV would be: (a) Utrecht-Rastadt, Ryswick, Nijmwegen, (b) Nijmwegen, Ryswick, Utrecht-Rastadt, (c) Ryswick, Nijmwegen, Aix-la-Chapelle, (d) Nijmwegen, Utrecht-Rastadt, Ryswick.

True-False

_____ 1. John Pym's "proposed departure from tradition" involved the question of control of England's army.

_____ 2. The alliance with Scottish Presbyterians and the reorganization of the army under Parliament assured the Puritan victory over Charles I.

_____ 3.   Charles II of England died a Roman Catholic.

_____ 4.   The English Toleration Act of 1689 granted religious freedom to all but the most radical religious groups.

_____ 5.   Despite his persecution of the Huguenots at home, Cardinal Richelieu allied France with Swedish Protestants during the Thirty Years' War.

_____ 6.   Throughout the seventeenth century Catholic Jansenists allied with the Jesuits against French Huguenots.

_____ 7.   Jean-Baptiste Colbert's economic policies had the effect of diminishing France's industrial and commercial potential.

_____ 8.   In reality the revocation of the Edict of Nantes came as a complete surprise.

_____ 9.   Philip of Anjou was the grandson of Louis XIV.

_____ 10.   From a military perspective England's success in the War of Spanish Succession was the result of excellent leadership and superior weapons.

Completion

1.   James VI of Scotland, who became James I of England, was the son of _____.

2.   The religious minister under Charles I was _____ and in the 1630s he provoked a war with Scotland.

3.   The largest military engagement of the English Civil War was the 1644 battle at _____.

4.   The fate of Charles I appears to have been sealed when Cromwell's New Model Army defeated him at _____ in June 1645.

5.   _____ was the official title used by Oliver Cromwell after taking power in 1653.

6.   The so-called "Glorious Revolution" in England was justified in the work titled _Second Treatise on Government_ written by _____.

7.   Primarily to build and maintain roads, an involuntary labor force was created in France in the seventeenth century by the introduction of the _____.

8.   Connecting the image of God to kings would be found in the writings of _____.

9.   The most famous of the defenders of the Jansenist movement was _____.

10.   _____ is the name used to describe the financial policies of the French minister Colbert.

7

CHAPTER 13
PATHS TO
CONSTITUTIONALISM AND
ABSOLUTISM: ENGLAND
AND FRANCE IN THE
SEVENTEENTH CENTURY

FOR FURTHER CONSIDERATION

1. English politics during the seventeenth century was a blend of religious concerns and monarchial decline. How does the reign of Elizabeth I in the previous century set the stage for the struggle between king and Parliament in this era?

2. What factors do you consider important in assessing the success of the Puritans during Cromwell's era?

3. Assess the roles of Cardinals Richelieu and Mazarin in the establishment of absolutism in France.

4. Examine the reign of Louis XIV. What were his successes and what were his failures?

5. Compare and contrast the development of the governments of England and France during the seventeenth century. Answer with specific references to persons, statutes, and events as needed.

ANSWERS

9

CHAPTER 13
PATHS TO
CONSTITUTIONALISM AND
ABSOLUTISM: ENGLAND
AND FRANCE IN THE
SEVENTEENTH CENTURY

Multiple-Choice

		Text Page
1.	A	307
2.	B	308
3.	B	309-310
4.	B	313
5.	D	314
6.	A	316
7.	C	321
8.	B	322
9.	C	325
10.	B	*passim*

True-False

1.	T	310
2.	T	311-312
3.	T	313
4.	F	314
5.	T	316
6.	F	321
7.	F	322
8.	F	324-325
9.	T	325
10.	T	325-326

Completion

1.	Mary Stuart, Queen of Scots	307
2.	William Laud	309
3.	Naseby	312
4.	Marston Moor	312
5.	Lord Protector	312
6.	John Locke	315
7	*corveé*	315
8	Bishop Bossuet	318
9.	Blaise Pascal	321
10.	Mercantilism	321

❖ ❖ ❖ ❖ ❖ ❖ ❖

New Directions in Thought and Culture in the Sixteenth and Seventeenth Centuries

Commentary

It is clear today that the discoveries initiated in the sixteenth century have ever since profoundly influenced Western thought. From the beginning, examination of the universe, particularly the study of the earth and the sun, was opening an entire new world to the people of the late Renaissance. This study was pioneered by men like Copernicus and Galileo. Through them a medieval concept of learning, rooted in the Scholastic concentration on past achievements, was replaced by a forward-looking emphasis on nature. For the comparatively few intellectuals and writers of these centuries this change meant charting new courses, whether in literature, which sought to entertain, or philosophy, which sought to answer, or politics, which sought to act and explain. A new intellectual synthesis had to be formed.

However the changeover from a medieval to a modern view was not devoid of, and in fact spurred an era of vicious assault on those whose views could not be readily explained. Unquestionably these attacks upon suspected witches, the vast majority of whom were middle aged and older women, were stimulated by religious warfare and the uncertainties created by intellectual fermentation.

Almost all of these writers deserve careful attention. The scientists like Galileo, Brahe, and Kepler were to apply mathematical reasoning to their studies of nature and the universe. Galileo's telescope was an important breakthrough itself even though some skeptics refused to look through it. Others, like Descartes and Newton, attempted to take the mathematical models even further along the path of human understanding. In their respective quests for truth, Descartes attempted to get a fresh intellectual start by beginning with only his own existence, and Newton established the basis of modern physics.

Great volumes of nationalist literature also appeared at this time as contemporary writers felt freer than ever before to explore human nature in all its ramifications. Cervantes in Spain and Shakespeare in England were dominant influences in this category. Other writers, like Milton and Bunyan, clearly reflected the political-religious struggle in England at the time.

Philosophy was also affected. The new approaches to nature could not help but trigger questions about the nature of God. Pascal's work, for example, drew upon the earlier and comparatively conservative views of John Calvin and St. Augustine. Spinoza's emphasis on God as embracing all of nature became in part the basis of a new Humanist religion.

During the seventeenth century a basic and what turned out to be a far-reaching reexamination of political philosophy took place. The resultant views reflected the new earthbound rationalism initiated by these early modern scientists. Thomas Hobbes and

John Locke, men of contrasting views, both lived through, and reflected on, turbulent political and religious times in England. Their works examined such basic concepts as the state of nature, the origin of state authority, and the social contract. As a result, their political works ever since have had a fundamental effect upon the political development of the West. Taken as a totality, these new intellectual directions brought to fruition and amplification ideas in science, technology, and philosophy that began with the Renaissance.

This Scientific Revolution, as it slowly unfolded for 150 years before the dawn of the eighteenth century, was an extensive and a most important development in the Western heritage.

IDENTIFICATIONS

Identify each one of the following as used in the text. Refer to text as necessary.

	Text Page
Scientific Revolution	330
Dialogues on the Two Chief Systems of the World	333
Principia Mathematica	335
malificium	336
"cunning folk"	336
Sancho Panza	338
William Shakespeare	339
Areopagitica	340
Paradise Lost	340
The Pilgrim's Progress	341
Discourse on Method	343
Pensées	344
Leviathan	345
"the desire for commodious living"	346
Anthony Ashley Cooper	346
Essay Concerning Human Understanding	347
Two Treatises on Government	347
Locke's "social contracts"	347

MAP EXERCISE A

Using the Copernican model, mark each of the known planets in its correct orbit. Note each planet's distance from the sun.

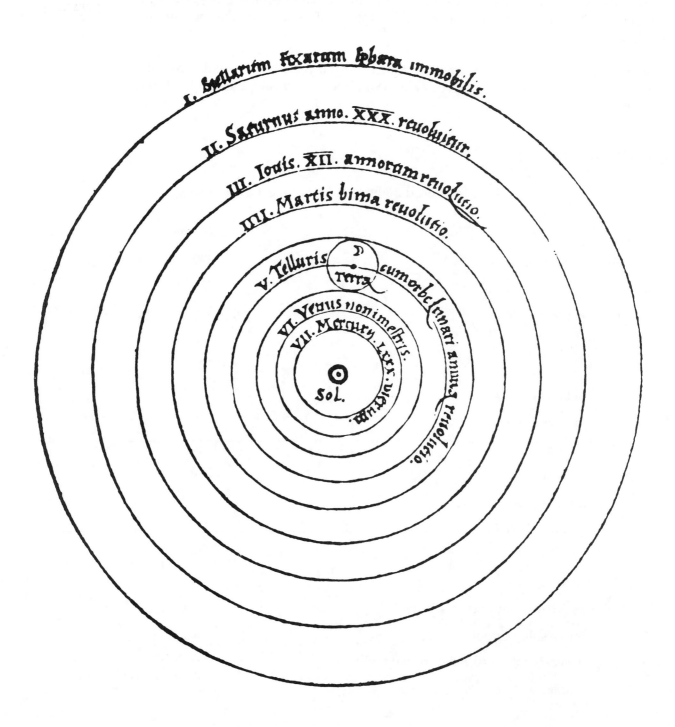

MAP EXERCISE B

In the approximately correct relationship to each other show the Sun, Earth, and the Moon. Indicate in miles and kilometers the exact distances between each. If possible, in days, how long would it take you to reach the Moon on a mountain bike, with a car, on a modern passenger jet, or a cruise ship?

SHORT-ANSWER EXERCISES

Multiple-Choice

_____ 1. Which of the following expressions best characterizes the nature of the Scientific Revolution? (a) it occurred several places in Europe at the same time, (b) it was not revolutionary in the normal sense of the word, (c) it grew out of the criticism associated with the Reformation, (d) all of these are correct.

_____ 2. Which of the following actually opposed Copernicus's views? (a) Tycho Brahe, (b) Johannes Kepler, (c) Galileo Galilei, (d) Francis Bacon.

_____ 3. The harmony between faith and science in this period is found in which of these views? (a) since nature is reasonable, God must be reasonable, (b) to study the laws of nature in reality is to study God, (c) faith and science are mutually supporting, (d) all of these.

_____ 4. During this era a classic argument for freedom of the press was written by: (a) Milton, (b) Shakespeare, (c) Cervantes, (d) Copernicus.

_____ 5. Which two of the following works most fervently expresses the idea of Puritan holiness? (a) *Grace Abounding*, (b) *Pilgrim's Progress*, (c) *Paradise Lost*, (d) *The Life and Death of Mr. Badman.*

_____ 6. Analytic geometry was first developed by: (a) Galileo, (b) Brahe, (c) Descartes, (d) none of these.

_____ 7. Pascal believed that: (a) there was danger in following traditional religious ways, (b) misery loves company, (c) God's mercy was for everyone, (d) it is better to believe in God than not to.

_____ 8. The most controversial thinker of the seventeenth century was: (a) René Descartes, (b) Blase Pascal, (c) Baruch Spinoza, (d) Thomas Hobbes.

_____ 9. In Thomas Hobbes's view, man was: (a) a person neither good nor evil, (b) a self-centered beast, (c) essentially God-fearing, (d) none of these.

_____ 10. Which of the following works was written first: (a) *On the Revolutions of Heavenly Spheres*, (b) *King Lear*, (c) *Leviathan*, (d) *Ethics.*

True-False

_____ 1. Nicolai Copernicus found the Ptolemaic system of the universe to be full of mathematical problems.

_____ 2. Middle aged and older women were particularly vulnerable during this era of witch hunts.

_____ 3. Don Quixote, Dulcinea, and Sancho Panza are all characters in Miguel de Cervantes' masterpiece.

_____ 4. The most original of Shakespeare's plays is *Hamlet*, which he produced in 1603.

_____ 5. In his work John Milton supported or defended each of the following: the execution of Charles I (1649), the right of divorce, freedom of the press, and Puritanism.

_____ 6. The Englishman Francis Bacon is considered to be the founder of the scientific method of research.

_____ 7. In 1632 René Descartes wrote *Dialogues on the Two Chief Systems of the World.*

_____ 8. The Jansenists believed in the original sinfulness of humans and their dependence on grace for salvation.

_____ 9. The Devil, lust, vanity, freedom, and death were each considered ingredients of Baruch Spinoza's new definitions.

_____ 10. Thomas Hobbes supported the idea of a strong and efficient ruler because he believed such a ruler would alleviate the dangers for humans existing in the state of nature.

Completion

1. The Ptolemaic view of the universe is found in a work written in the second century and titled the _____.

2. The work of _____ expanded on the previous efforts of Nicolaus Copernicus and Tycho Brahe.

3. For Galileo the rationality for the entire universe was based on _____.

4. The power of the Catholic Church and the Inquisition largely prevented the Protestant Reformation from coming to _____.

5. As a young man, _____ was decorated for gallantry in the great naval battle of Lepanto.

6. The author of the story in which the characters journey to the Celestial City is _____.

7. Perfecting the microscope is usually associated with the work of _____ and _____ .

8. The political philosopher Thomas Hobbes believed that the dangers of _____ were greater than the dangers of tyranny.

9. _____ was the author of *Patriarcha, or the Natural Power of Kings*.

10. _____ believed that human ruling went beyond control of the jungle of selfish egomaniacs; it required the ruler to preserve the law of nature.

FOR FURTHER CONSIDERATION

1. Describe the roles of Nicolaus Copernicus and Francis Bacon in influencing what is now referred to as the Scientific Revolution.

2. What was the new world view worked out during this era? How did it differ from the medieval view? What effects did the new concept of the universe have on all of the sciences?

3. How were the lives of Miguel de Cervantes and William Shakespeare different? What effect did their experiences have on their writing? Cite specific examples.

4. Discuss the central characteristics of the thought of Thomas Hobbes. Are there parts of his work that are reflected in modern times?

5. Contrast Hobbes's view of authority with that of John Locke. Why is Locke considered so influential even in modern times?

ANSWERS

Multiple-Choice

		Text Page
1.	D	330-333
2.	A	331
3.	D	335
4.	A	340
5.	A and B	341
6.	C	343
7.	D	344
8.	C	344
9.	B	346
10.	A	*passim*

True-False

1.	T	331
2.	T	337
3.	T	338
4.	F	339
5.	T	340
6.	T	341
7.	F	343
8.	T	344
9.	F	345
10.	T	346

Completion

1.	*Almagest*	330
2.	Johannes Kepler	332
3.	mathematics	333
4.	Spain	338
5.	Miguel de Cervantes	338
6.	John Bunyan	341
7.	Robert Hooke/ Anton von Leeuwenhoek	342
8.	anarchy	346
9.	Sir Robert Filmer	347
10.	John Locke	347

SUCCESSFUL AND UNSUCCESSFUL PATHS TO POWER (1686-1740)

COMMENTARY

The end of the seventeenth and the early part of the eighteenth century were a period of state building. While perhaps not in the modern sense of nation building, wherein the role of the ordinary citizen would become a factor, it was in the sense of building the state organizational structure. The role of an increasingly international economy and empire building in the Americas contributed to the necessity of new infrastructures. The Reformation itself, the religiously inspired warfare that followed, and such great wars as the Thirty Years' War (1618-1648) and the Great Northern War (1700-1721), clearly undermined the medieval nature of state systems. The intellectual achievements of the so-called Scientific Revolution had profoundly altered views on how states might be governed. The initial decades of the eighteenth century provided an opportunity for states to catch up on their own internal development. At the same time the stage was being set for more dramatic changes at the end of the century.

As a result of internal reforms, certain Western European states were placed on the road to modernity whereas other states languished by the end of the century. England was to remain in the forefront of political and economic development, while in Brandenburg-Prussia (the future Germany) and in the Russia of Peter the Great important steps would be taken that would have far-reaching impact on both nations' future development. Within the general framework of change in governmental structure and reform several distinct developments were taking place.

The positions of Spain and the Netherlands would wane in the eighteenth century. In France the absolutism so ruthlessly established in the previous century would be streamlined, and though corrupted, would remain well entrenched in the French system. In England the influence of Parliament would grow, placing that country on the road to liberal reform and, ultimately, to industrial growth. Further eastward in Europe, nations appeared to be developing modern state systems largely through the dominating personalities of monarchs like Frederick William, the Great Elector of Prussia, his son Frederick William I, and Peter the Great of Russia. Despite the efforts of the Hapsburg emperor of Austria, Charles VI, his lack of a male successor to the throne weakened that ancient Catholic monarchy. Russian entrance into the European arena reflected the troubled and often ambivalent relationship that nation had maintained with Western states for centuries. This era witnessed a decline of Sweden, Poland, and the Ottoman Empire. Notable also during this era was the increasing importance of overseas empires that served to support their "mother" states in Europe. In empire-building, too, at least for a time, France and England would enjoy a distinct advantage.

More clearly, by the mid-eighteenth century several of the European states were destined for second-class status, whereas others, because of a confluence of factors, were able to better themselves. Although these developments did not reach a climax in this era, the world stage was being set for a great power struggle in the period from 1750 through the age of Napoleon, ending in 1815.

IDENTIFICATIONS

Identify each one of the following as used in the text. Refer to the text as necessary.

	Text Page
John Law	351
parlements	352
South Sea Company	354
"Let sleeping dogs lie"	354
Great Northern War	357
zimmis	358
"exploding" the Diet	359
Magyars	359
Pragmatic Sanction	360
The Great Elector	361-363
Junkers	361
Frederick William I	363
"Time of Troubles"	364
Mikhail Romanov	364
boyers and *streltsy*	364-466
Table of Ranks	366
Old Believers Movement	366
Saint Petersburg	367

Map Exercise A

Locate and mark the boundaries of those states that border the Austrian Empire.

Trace the Danube River through the Austrian Empire.

Locate each of the following cities:

1.	Vienna	4.	Lemberg
2.	Budapest	5.	Belgrade
3.	Prague	6.	Mohacs

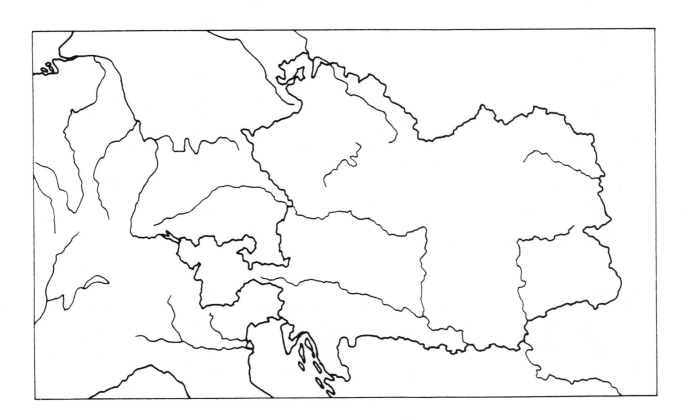

Map Exercise B

Outline each of the following countries/areas: Sweden, Finland and Russia.

Locate the cities of Stockholm, St. Petersburg, Moscow, and Helsinki.

Mark the Baltic Sea, Lake Ladoga, and the Gulf of Finland.

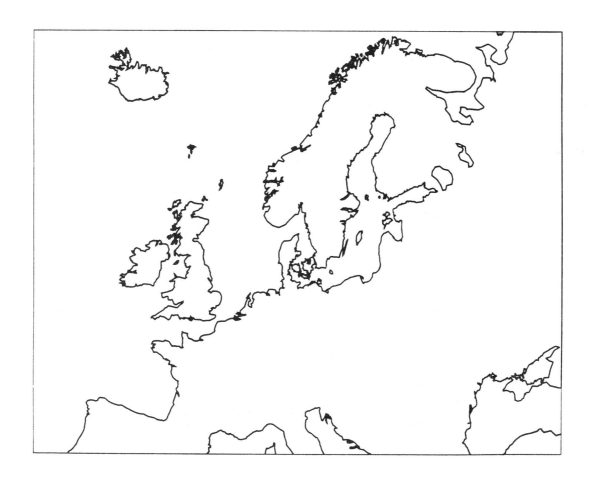

Short-Answer Exercises

Multiple-Choice

_____ 1. According to the text, which of the following countries was not moving forward in this period? (a) Great Britain, (b) Russia, (c) Spain, (d) Prussia.

_____ 2. Which of the following contributed *least* to the decline of the Netherlands in the eighteenth century? (a) the fishing industry, (b) shipbuilding, (c) the financial community, (d) various domestic industries.

_____ 3. The Mississippi Company: (a) after earlier troubles operated profitably, (b) was responsible for the management of the French national debt, (c) ended the financial career of John Law, (d) all of these.

_____ 4. During the eighteenth century the English Parliament was dominated by: (a) the old aristocracy, (b) the rising middle class, (c) owners of property, (d) representatives of the people.

_____ 5. As one moved farther eastward in Europe in the eighteenth century there was increasing likelihood of finding: (a) rotten boroughs, (b) serfdom, (c) prominent intellectuals, (d) larger navies.

_____ 6. During this period of time Sweden's weakness was in her: (a) economy, (b) army, (c) location on the Baltic Sea, (d) none of these.

_____ 7. In the early eighteenth century a major defeat of Sweden occurred in the battle of: (a) Poltava, (b) Regensburg, (c) Narva, (d) none of these.

_____ 8. Beginning in this era a major factor in European international relations was the decline of: (a) the Ottoman Empire, (b) Poland, (c) Russia, (d) Austria.

_____ 9. The General-Ober-Finanz-Kriegs-und-Domänen-Direktorium is normally associated with the state of: (a) Russia, (b) Poland, (c) Prussia, (d) the Holy Roman Empire.

_____ 10. Which of the following occurred first? (a) Russia defeated in the battle at Narva, (b) European tour of Peter the Great, (c) Saint Petersburg founded, (d) end of the Great Northern War.

True-False

_____ 1. By relying on imports of precious metals from the New World the government of Spain was able to successfully stimulate that nation's overall economic development.

_____ 2. The chief feature of French political life in the eighteenth century until the French Revolution (1789) was the attempt of the nobility to limit monarchial power.

_____ 3. Louis XV of France is considered a failure not only because of his mediocrity but that he was never properly trained as a ruler, was lazy and given to vice.

_____ 4. Both Whigs and Tories were proponents of the status quo in England, yet the Tories supported urban commercial interests and were in favor of religious toleration in general.

_____ 5. Robert Walpole's success resulted from his careful use of government patronage and manipulation of the House of Commons.

_____ 6. By the end of the seventeenth century, warfare and the resultant shifting political loyalties had become basic ingredients of life in central Europe.

_____ 7. The Pragmatic Sanction was designed to insure the succession to the Austrian throne of Maria Theresa.

_____ 8.   Frederick II (Hohenzollern) of Prussia married Maria Theresa (Habsburg) of Austria to insure his title to the lands of Prussia.

_____ 9.   As a result of frequent revolutions, military conspiracies, and assassinations the Romanov's only ruled Russia for 100 years.

_____ 10.   By the middle of the eighteenth century Russia was Europe's largest producer of iron.

Completion

1. The Treaty of _____ established a French interest in the Spanish monarchy.

2. Though not having the power to legislate, the _____ of France became effective centers of resistance to royal authority.

3. The most influential minister in the reign of France's Louis XV was the aged _____.

4. In reality _____ could be considered the first Prime Minister of Great Britain.

5. By laying siege to the city of _____ in 1683 the Turks were able to demonstrate the power of the Ottoman Empire.

6. The _liberum veto_ was a practice exercised in the central legislative assembly of _____.

7. The rise of the Hohenzollern family to control of Prussia began with their rule of the German territory of _____.

8. _____ were the important class of German nobility influential throughout Prussian history.

9. In 1722 Peter the Great attempted to rearrange the Russian nobility through the _____.

10. An early attempt at religious reform in Russia was led by the Patriarch _____.

FOR FURTHER CONSIDERATION

1. Describe the development of parliamentary government in England in the first half of the eighteenth century. What kind of compromises made this unique system work?

2. Looking at the history of the Ottoman Empire (modern Turkey), what does the text see as the causes of the "political and ethnic turmoil that still continues" to this day?

3. How does the development of central authority in Prussia differ from that in other European states during this period? How was it similar?

4. Why were the so-called "reform" efforts of Russia's Peter the Great successful only in part?

5. Generally characterize the differences between the Eastern European States [Sweden, Poland, Austria, Prussia, and Russia] and the Western states [France and England].

ANSWER

Multiple-Choice

		Text Page
1.	C	349
2.	C	351
3.	D	351
4.	C	354
5.	B	357
6.	A	357
7.	A	357
8.	A	358
9.	C	363
10.	B	365

True-False

1.	F	350
2.	T	352
3.	T	352
4.	F	353
5.	T	354
6.	T	357
7.	T	360
8.	F	361
9.	F	364
10.	T	367

Completion

1.	Utrecht	350
2.	*parlements*	352
3.	Cardinal Fleury	352
4.	Robert Walpole	354
5.	Vienna	358
6.	Poland	359
7.	Brandenburg	361
8.	Junkers	361-362
9.	Table of Ranks	366
10.	Nikon	366

◆ ◆ ◆ ◆ ◆ ◆ ◆

FOR FURTHER CONSIDERATION OF THE DOCUMENTS

Each of the following questions is designed to help you reach a better understanding of the original documents presented in the last five chapters of the text. Feel free to use the page numbers provided to refer back to the document as necessary. The value of a primary historical source should not be underestimated; it helps us understand the nature of the era in which it was written.

Luther on Justification by Faith (p. 258)
1. Explain what is being "justified?" How does Luther arrive at "faith alone?" What are your views on Luther and eternity?

The Right to Resist Tyranny (p. 287)
2. Though more often stated in later centuries, Theodore Beza touches upon a basic premise respective to the origin of authority within a state which is fundamental to Western political thought. Explain this premise fully.

Bossuet on the Divine Right of Kings (p. 318)
3. What was the basis of Bossuet's defense of the concept of divine right? What are your views on the origin of government authority?

Galileo Discusses Science and the Bible (pp. 332-333)
4. How do Galileo's arguments hold up in light of similar debates today which center around the role of God in the world, particularly since Darwin (1859)?

Lady Montagu's Advice on Election to Parliament (p. 356)
5. What does this letter suggest about the role of women of high birth in the eighteenth century?

SOCIETY AND ECONOMICS UNDER THE OLD REGIME IN THE EIGHTEENTH CENTURY

COMMENTARY

The *old regime* is a generally descriptive term applied to life in Europe before the French Revolution. Used in this way, the term covers practically every facet of European social, economic, and political development before 1789.

Nowhere was the inherent harshness of the old regime experienced more than among the poorer classes, which under a variety of names worked the land or peopled the least savory areas of the urban landscape. Though conditions varied throughout Europe, peasants on the land or in the cities suffered at the hands of tyrannical landlords, oppressive styles of government, and a routinely harsh daily life. This situation did not suddenly improve with the development of the so-called "Agricultural Revolution." On the contrary, the initial advances brought on by the increased agricultural output favored the landlords and the middlemen instead of the persons working the land.

Increasingly, records from this era allow today's student to gain considerable insight into eighteenth-century social development. The emergence of modern, or at least premodern, household patterns can be detected. Similarly, the role of women, servants, and children can be viewed as important ingredients in preindustrial society. It should be clear that the position of these persons was rarely easy.

An additional pressure on eighteenth-century life was the growth in population that took place throughout the 1700s. Societies today are better able to monitor population growth; but in the eighteenth century, demography (the study of population's shift, growth, decline, and statistics) was an unknown science. The effects of this population growth were similar to the effects of population growth in our time. Although governments and their people remained largely unaware of the phenomenon, demographic development was greatly to affect all areas of European life.

Simultaneous with the growth of population and improved agricultural techniques came the earliest stages of modern industrial development. In fact among historians and graduate students of our day in the United States, Europe and elsewhere there is an emerging field of studies under the name proto-industrialization. Students are examining the earliest stages of the phenomenon that became the Industrial Revolution. This "Revolution" began in earnest during the eighteenth century, and its effects have continued to be felt to the present day. This period of industrialization was not really revolutionary in the modern sense of the term, but rather was the result of a series of historic and mechanical developments that combined in this century to change forever the character of Western life. The early inventions, coupled with the entrepreneurial spirit of the time, led to the development of capitalist traditions and principles now widely accepted. It is not surprising that Great Britain was the first nation to advance as a result of industrialization.

Despite these changes in the economic character of European life, the position of the aristocracy remained powerful and largely tax exempt. True, the position of the nobility varied from country to country according to past traditions and was weighted directly in proportion to the strength of the ruling monarch. Throughout the eighteenth century the aristocracy would remain the most influential force in European society and was in many instances the controlling one. In retrospect the nobility of western Europe, especially in Great Britain, would appear to be more receptive to change than were their eastern European counterparts. As industrial developments brought economic and commercial benefits to the cities many aristocrats were quick to cash in on these advances. Because of their inherited control over the political system, they were normally able to make things work toward their own benefit. At the same time the aristocracy was being challenged by a relatively new class of urban dwellers who were not definable within the traditional framework of upper or lower class.

This middle group was clearly committed to industrialization and the commercial advantages to be achieved through it. Their position within the world of commerce was important because here the middle class could stimulate industrial growth and further profit from industrial output. The *bourgeoisie,* or middle class, could be found in all cities large and small. They were the new and vital ingredient of the commercial-industrial revolution of the eighteenth century. Driven by the motives of profit, success, and social acceptance its individuals were soon to form the vanguard of change into the modern era. They were the most dynamic of all the classes in this century. They remained above the artisan and poorer classes of the city in wealth and prestige and enjoyed an increasing ability to control their own lives.

The artisan class was made up of a diverse group of trades-people and shopkeepers. Their activities were an important part of emerging urban life. They performed the sometimes small but necessary everyday services that allowed those who were socially and economically above them to function and, in a sense, those below them to survive. The role of this artisan class should be noted in the ritualized phenomenon of the "bread riot."

The workers and urban poor remained at the bottom of the eighteenth-century social and economic ladder. Their life, far more than that of the other classes, was harsh. No one could truly escape the filth and brutality of eighteenth-century life, but these people—and they were the majority—were constantly and most directly affected by it.

At the close of the eighteenth century, society was already beginning to take on the tempo of nineteenth- and twentieth-century societies. Yet many aspects of the old regime remained. In short, society in this era can be viewed as turning from the certainty of the past to the uncertainty of the uncharted future—a future of which you and I today are the products.

IDENTIFICATIONS

Identify each one of the following as used in the text. Refer to the text as necessary.

	Text Page
ancien régime	369
aristocratic resurgence	371
hobereaux	372
corveés	372
banalitiés	373
servants	374
coitis interruptus	378
infanticide	379
crop rotation	380
Industrial Revolution	382
Josiah Wedgwood	383
domestic system	385
James Hargreaves	385
James Watt	386
"just price"	390
"riff-raff"	391
"court Jews"	391

MAP EXERCISE A

Outline/locate each of the following on the accompanying map:

Countries	Capital Cities	Water Bodies/Rivers
1. England	9. London	17. Thames
2. Scotland	10. Edinburgh	18. Firth of Forth
3. Ireland	11. Dublin	19. Irish Sea
4. France	12. Paris	20. Seine
5. Prussia	13. Berlin	21. Oder
6. Poland	14. Warsaw	22. Vistula
7. Austria	15. Vienna	23. Danube
8. Russia	16. Saint Petersburg	24. Gulf of Finland

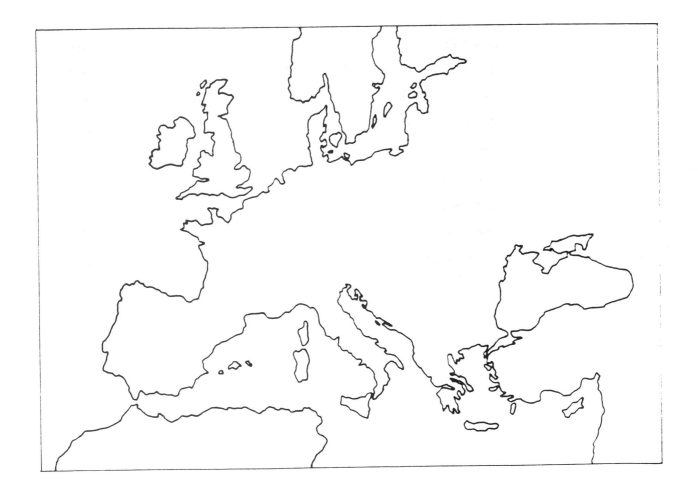

GRAPH EXERCISE B

Referring to the statistics presented on p. 381 of the text, prepare a graph (or spreadsheet) demonstrating the growth of European population from 1700 to 1850. To enhance your understanding of the demographics of this era, research similar statistics for the thirteen British colonies in North America that became the United States during this same period.

countries

1700   1850

SHORT-ANSWER EXERCISES

33
CHAPTER 16
SOCIETY AND ECONOMICS
UNDER THE OLD REGIME
IN THE
18TH CENTURY

Multiple-Choice

_____ 1. According to the textbook the old regime was characterized by all of the following except: (a) absolute monarchy, (b) an agrarian economy, (c) aristocratic elites, (d) Protestant domination.

_____ 2. The leadership within the British aristocracy was composed of approximately: (a) 200, (b) 400, (c) 600, (d) 800 families.

_____ 3. In which of the following places did the nobility reckon their wealth in "souls:" (a) Russia, (b) Poland, (c) Austria, (d) Heaven.

_____ 4. Which of the following developed techniques that moved cotton production from the home to the factory: (a) Richard Arkwright, (b) Henry Cort, (c) Edmund Cartwright, (d) James Hargreaves.

_____ 5. Population growth during the eighteenth century appears to be caused mainly by all of the following except: (a) fewer wars and epidemics, (b) better medical knowledge and techniques, (c) a decline in the death rate, (d) changes in the supply and quality of food.

_____ 6. During this century which of the following was not a contributing factor to Britain's industrial development: (a) generally low taxes, (b) highly stratified class structure, (c) rich deposits of coal and iron, (d) few internal trade barriers.

_____ 7. The machine most responsible for bringing about the combination of industrialization with urbanization was the: (a) power loom, (b) flying shuttle, (c) steam engine, (d) spinning jenny.

_____ 8. Surprisingly, in this era poverty was: (a) worse in the cities, (b) considered a crime, (c) almost nonexistent, (d) worse in the countryside.

_____ 9. Which of the following statements is most correct about the emerging middle class in Europe: (a) the land was not a primary source of middle class income, (b) they feared the lower classes, (c) they lived chiefly in the towns and cities, (d) all of these are correct statements about the middle class of this era.

_____ 10. Which of the following is least correct about eighteenth century society: (a) it was on the brink of considerable economic, social, and political change, (b) scarcity remained a major problem throughout western Europe, (c) the growth of population was affecting most areas of European life, (d) there was a growing willingness among all the classes to seek innovative solutions to all the problems confronted.

True-False

_____ 1. Oddly, in their desire to maintain traditional rights both 18th-century peasants and aristocrats sought to protect existing privileges.

_____ 2. At this time approximately 95% of the populations of the various European countries would be considered non-aristocratic.

_____ 3. The practice of young men and women moving away from home was known as neocolonialism.

_____ 4. In non-aristocratic households the males were expected to do virtually all the work of the family unit.

_____ 5. The eighteenth century saw a stabilization of the numbers of children admitted to foundling homes.

_____ 6. Though upsetting the political structure, industrialization permitted greater control over the forces of nature than had ever been possible before.

_____ 7. Edmund Cartwright developed the power loom in the 1780's.

_____ 8. Generally, the emerging middle class feared those below them and resented those above them in society.

_____ 9. A change in clothing prices is generally considered the most common spark to urban riots in this era.

_____ 10. As we know it today, the desire to make money and accumulate profits, the so-called "commercial spirit," really began in the eighteenth century.

Completion

1. Eighteenth-century French aristocracy was basically divided into the nobility of the _____ and the nobility of the _____.

2. Though enjoying many privileges the French nobility were liable for a tax known as the _____ .

3. _____ constituted the economic basis of eighteenth-century life.

4. The great peasant uprising in Russia during the reign of Catherine the Great was led by _____.

5. The first practical steam engine was invented by _____.

6. The new puddling process, which vastly improved the qualities of the iron produced, was developed by _____.

7. During the eighteenth-century Europe's most populous city was _____.

8. The engravings of _____ portray the problems caused by urbanization in London during the mid-eighteenth century.

9. Urban _____ during this era were generally well-organized actions against price increases in food.

10. Throughout the era of the old regime European _____ were considered socially and religiously inferior.

FOR FURTHER CONSIDERATION

1. Generally describe the operation of the eighteenth-century nonaristocratic family. How did servants fit into this pattern? Fully describe the role of women in, and without, a family. How did preteen children fit into the world you have described?

2. Discuss the Enclosure Movement in Great Britain. What exactly was involved when land was enclosed? What were the advantages and disadvantages of a land enclosure program?

3. A number of newly invented machines were fundamental to the early stages of industrialization. What were these machines and in what way(s) were they improvements over the previous method of production? How did these machines actually work, and what specific effect did each have on a given process?

4. Why was the comparatively small middle class considered the most dynamic of the eighteenth-century urban classes?

5. To what would you attribute the striking contrast between urban rich and the urban poor in the eighteenth century? How do the distinctions between them reflect the overall problem of urban life then and now?

ANSWERS

Multiple-Choice

		Text Page
1.	D	369
2.	B	371
3.	A	373
4.	B	381
5.	A	384
6.	A	385
7.	C	386
8.	D	388
9.	D	389
10.	B	392

True-False

1.	T	370
2.	T	370
3.	F	375
4.	F	378
5.	F	379
6.	T	382
7.	T	385
8.	T	389
9.	F	390
10.	T	392

True-False

1.	sword/robe	371
2.	*vingtieme*/twentieth	372
3.	land	372
4.	Emelyan Pugachev	374
5.	Thomas Newcomen	386
6.	Henry Cort	386
7.	London	387
8.	William Hogarth	388
9.	riots	390
10.	Jews	391

◆ ◆ ◆ ◆ ◆ ◆ ◆

EMPIRE, WAR, AND COLONIAL REBELLION

COMMENTARY

By the eighteenth century, wars fought exclusively for religious ideals were a thing of the past. What emerged in this century was a competition among the European states for control of areas on the continent, North America, and elsewhere throughout the world. Because of the Europeans' wealth and technological superiority, in the sixteenth and seventeenth centuries they were able to conquer their overseas empires and in the eighteenth century expand them. From the European perspective the world was there for the taking. Nor did the captains of industry and commerce and the leaders of governments shrink from these opportunities. It is in this context that the importation and exploitation of vast numbers of slaves began. Quickly the trade in African blacks mushroomed into a major Atlantic commercial operation. Considerable profits were gained by local colonial planters, by those actually engaged in the slave trade, and by many others connected to the enterprise. Though not clearly understood, and perhaps, not fully defined until the end of the century, mercantilism was meant to be the operative principle between home states and their colonies. Spain, France, and England by diverse means attempted to maintain a favorable balance of trade with their respective colonies. Initially, accumulation of gold and silver was the determinant of success. However, as the colonies in North America began to compete with English home-based products a movement, not unique to England, to control trade within the empire developed. For England and France this mercantile competition led to an enlarged confrontation complicated this time by new European alliances. The ensuing struggles, which culminated in the great wars at mid-century, can be divided into two broad categories: Prussia's challenge to Austria's influence in central Europe; and a colonial rivalry between England and France. And despite Spain's efforts to maintain political and economic control over her Latin America possessions, England and France sought to take advantage of apparent Spanish weaknesses. When these conflicts were ended with the treaties of Hubertusberg and Paris in 1763, all the participating powers were still left standing; but all had been badly shaken by the length, violence, and cost of the wars. These intensified rivalries left Austria and France especially weakened—Austria in prestige and France in colonial influence.

Prussia's initial difficulties in the contest had been turned into success and that nation was thereby placed among the great powers of Europe. In England's successful bid for North American supremacy, however, lay the seeds of the struggle for American independence. The vast territories held by France were handed over to England with the peace. Yet, the French-British rivalry continued and was given new expression during the American War for Independence. The taxation necessary in Great Britain and her North American possessions to pay for the war and for the enlarged costs of administering the newly won territories was a direct and fundamental cause of the American revolt against Great Britain. The Americans simply could not accept Parliament's interpretation of what was now necessary for the British Empire. Long isolated from their brethren in England, the Americans had adopted a self-assured attitude and viewpoint that envisioned their own future free of London interference. By employing arguments that had influenced British political thought over the previous one hundred years, and by steadfastly refusing to submit to British authority, they soon drew the issue between "mother" and "daughter" states. By the spring of 1775 the colonies had organized and begun to marshal public opinion against George III's government. In the accompanying pamphleteering, Thomas Paine's *Common Sense* enlarged the view that separation was the answer. After eight years of intermittent fighting, a second Peace of Paris (1783) recognized the independence of Britain's former seaboard colonies as the United States of America. Having declared their independence in 1776 these areas were free to experiment with political, social, and economic activities unheard of in previous centuries. These experiments, some successful, reflected the thinking of the time, the Enlightenment, and also the unique character of American frontier life. The ideas they embodied have become part of the Western heritage.

IDENTIFICATIONS

Identify each one of the following as used in the text. Refer to the text as necessary.

	Text page
mercantilism	396
Treaty of Utrecht	402-403
asiento	403
Convention of Westminster	405
Prince Kaunitz	405
Treaty of Hubertusberg	405
Pitt the Elder	405
Battle of Plassey	406
Treaty of Paris (1763)	406
Charles Townshend	408
Lord North	409
Quebec Act	409
Treaty of Paris (1783)	409
The Commonwealthmen	410
John Wilkes	410
Christopher Wyvil	412
Pitt the Younger	412

MAP EXERCISE A

Locate each of the following on the accompanying map:

1. Colonial Empire of Great Britain before 1763
2. Colonial Empire of France before 1763
3. Colonial Empire of Spain
4. Dutch colonies in the New World
5. The West Indies

MAP EXERCISE B

On this map of the eastern seaboard of North America, mark each of the thirteen British colonies founded there after 1607. Mark the largest city (town) in each in the year 1776.

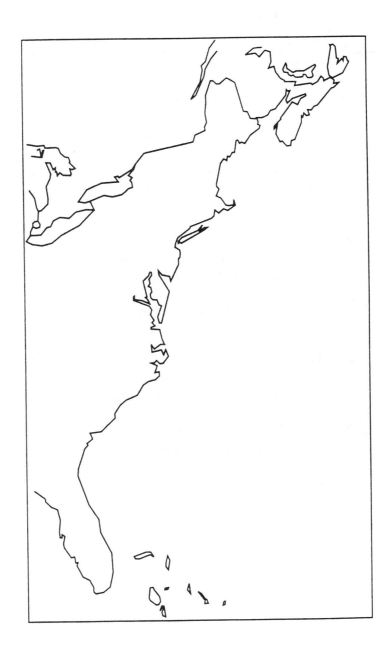

SHORT-ANSWER EXERCISES

Multiple-Choice

_____ 1. European contacts with the rest of the world have passed through how many distinct stages? (a) 3, (b) 4, (c) 5, (d) 6.

_____ 2. The European dominance of the world was based on: (a) location, (b) cultural superiority, (c) technological advances, (d) none of these were factors.

_____ 3. The most influential part of Spain's efforts to regulate trade with her possessions in the New World was the: (a) viceroys, (b) *flota* system, (c) *Casa de Contratación*, (d) Peninsulares.

_____ 4. Which of the following cities was not a center of the Atlantic slave trade? (a) Amsterdam, Netherlands, (b) Liverpool, England, (c) Newport, Rhode Island, (d) Nantes, France.

_____ 5. Empress Maria Theresa's arrangement with the: (a) Prussians, (b) Turks, (c) Poles, (d) Magyars, preserved the state in the eighteenth century but actually hampered later development.

_____ 6. Which of the following treaties was negotiated first: (a) Treaty of Paris, (b) Treaty of Aix-la-Chapelle, (c) Treaty of Westphalia, (d) Treaty of Utrecht.

_____ 7. The root cause of the American colonial revolt against Great Britain was concern over: (a) imperial taxation, (b) imperial policy toward the western lands, (c) imperial control of colonial finances, (d) all of these.

_____ 8. Initially, the Second Continental Congress was: (a) belligerent, (b) promonarchy, (c) conciliatory, (d) none of these.

_____ 9. Which of the following documents had the most effect on the American struggle for independence? (a) *The Treaty of Paris*, (b) *Convention of Westminster*, (c) *Common Sense*, (d) *Cato's Letters*.

_____ 10. Which of the following is most correct about the American Revolution: (a) slaves were freed, (b) it was truly a radical revolution, (c) its ideas were limited to North America, (d) it encouraged socialism.

True-False

_____ 1. Armies were the most important feature of eighteenth-century mercantile empires.

_____ 2. Joseph Dupleix and Robert Clive are both important names associated with the European colonization efforts in India.

_____ 3. For Spain the governmental structure in the colonies was designed to augment commercial goals.

_____ 4.   Generally speaking, most laws governing slavery were designed to protect those held in bondage from the excessive cruelties of their masters.

_____ 5.   In reality, the British right secured in the Treaty of Utrecht to send one ship per year to the great trading fair at Portobello, Panama opened the door to vast smuggling opportunities.

_____ 6.   The real surprise in the so-called "diplomatic revolution" was the British-French settlement of outstanding colonial differences.

_____ 7.   Throughout his career Count Anton Kaunitz, the Austrian foreign minister, was determined to maintain a German-based alliance with Prussia.

_____ 8.   The 1773 Tea Act that triggered the Boston Tea Party actually had lowered the price of tea for the colonies.

_____ 9.   The governments right of taxation, the arbitrary power of the monarchy, and the perceived corruption of the House of Commons were all factors influencing American opinion on the eve of the War of Independence.

_____ 10. The American revolution should be viewed, not only as a movement for colonial independence, but one destined to eventually shape the world that followed.

Completion

1. Virtually all the colonial powers had possessions in the _____ Sea.

2. The governing principle behind all colonization in this era was the theory of _____.

3. A shortage of _____ was a driving force in the slave trade.

4. One of the more unusual aspects of Great Britain's rivalry with Spain during this period was a 1739 conflict known as the War of _____.

5. Britain's victories in Europe and North America were engineered by Secretary of State _____.

6. The British ministry under George Grenville passed the _____ Act which was symbolic of Britain's need for additional revenue.

7. The _____ crisis set the stage for years of struggle between Britain and her American colonies, finally leading to the latter's independence.

8. Political theory that inspired the successful American drive for independence can be found in the 17th century struggle in England against the _____.

9. _____ was the English monarch throughout the period of the American revolution.

10. Internal opposition to the king of Great Britain can be associated with the group known as the _____.

For Further Consideration

1. Describe the mercantile empires of the major European states. What was the particular colonial or economic value of each area?

2. Define mercantilism and give several eighteenth-century examples of the practice.

3. Describe the development of slavery in the New World during this era. Can you distinguish between Spanish and English usage of Africans in their respective colonial empires? Why was France less involved in the slave trade than the other major competitors for the Empire in the New World?

4. Discuss several factors of British life in the 1750s and 1760s which in your opinion were stimulants to the rebellion in North America.

5. Can you relate the Association Movement in England to the American Revolution? Use specific examples as necessary to support your answer.

Multiple-Choice

		Text Page
1.	B	395
2.	B	395
3.	C	397
4.	A	401
5.	D	404
6.	C	*passim*
7.	D	407-409
8.	C	409
9.	C	409
10.	B	413

True-False

1.	F	395
2.	T	397
3.	T	397
4.	F	401
5.	T	403
6.	F	405
7.	F	405
8.	T	409
9.	T	411
10.	T	413

Completion

1.	Caribbean	396
2.	mercantilism	396
3.	labor	400
4.	Jenkins's Ear	403
5.	William Pitt, the Elder	405-406
6.	Sugar	407
7.	Stamp Act	408
8.	Stuarts	409
9.	George III	410
10.	Whigs	410

The Age of Enlightenment: Eighteenth-Century Thought

Commentary

The *Enlightenment* is the broad term applied to the intellectual developments of the eighteenth century. These developments were sponsored by a relatively small number of thinkers and writers primarily throughout western Europe. Their work and thoughts set the stage for much of our thinking today. What these philosophers advocated were related ideas in two areas: personal freedoms and the reform of existing conditions and institutions. By so doing they provided an important part of the background for the many social, political, and economic changes that occurred in this era.

Although the seeds for much of the Enlightenment's emphasis can be found in the moderate political and social atmosphere of England, France was the heart of the movement. French writers such as Voltaire and Montesquieu were pioneers in championing Enlightenment ideas. By the middle of the eighteenth century reformers were sharpening their criticism and pointing increasingly to specific problems within the *ancien régime*.

With a new definition of the role of nature in human life the *philosophes* proposed changes in most aspects of existence. The increased knowledge at their disposal, as exemplified by the *Encyclopedia*, made them confident that their reforms were both reasonable and possible. Increased knowledge and rationality, the reformers hoped, would be the keys to both the immediate and the long-range effects of their work.

In a number of areas one can trace the thoughts of the eighteenth-century intellectuals. The concept of deism, for example, provided a means by which thinkers could accept the new rationalism without specifically denying the role of the supernatural (God) in human life. The organized religions, however, especially the Catholic Church, were being held up to considerable ridicule stemming from the *philosophes'* view of the medieval nature of religion. The rationalists of the eighteenth century were not prepared to accept what they believed to be the oppressive and irrational views of the Roman Church. At the same time the *philosophes* called for and supported a greater degree of religious toleration for all the faiths of Europe.

The effect of the Enlightenment on society was to be profound. Its thinkers insisted that, like nature itself, society must be founded on a rational base. Where it was not, then changes, reforms, must be instituted. The humane considerations of Beccaria and Bentham should be noted in this regard. The attention given to economic systems by prominent Enlightenment thinkers should also be observed. Adam Smith's position raised many new questions about the existing mercantile practices of the time and remained the philosophical basis for much of this period of industrialization. His work has remained fundamental to Western society's debate over economic progress and individual well-being.

It is in the area of political thought that the *philosophes* have continued to have the greatest impact right to the present day. Not since the ancient Greeks had the foundations of the systems by which human beings have governed themselves been opened to so much investigation and criticism. The *philosophes,* in sometimes widely varying approaches, were attempting to find the rationality behind Europe's governmental systems and in so doing they became involved in discussions and advocated changes that cut across the social and political base of existing institutions. Going well beyond mere criticism of corruption in government and church, the *philosophes* sought to establish a new set of fundamentals by which human beings could reasonably be governed in the future. Many writers such as Rousseau were vague as to how their new systems would work but were surely suggesting radically different approaches. Montesquieu, on the other hand, outlined a system calling for a division of political authority between three distinct branches of government. Interestingly, it was Rousseau's assertions that women belong at home; their main responsibility was to please men he argued. This position brought the condemnation of men and Enlightenment thought associated with the works of Mary Wollstonecraft.

The way in which these ideas reached into eastern Europe was in the form of Enlightened Absolutism. With this principle the rulers of Prussia, Austria, and Russia attempted to strengthen their monarchial grasp by utilizing select Enlightenment principles to their own advantage. Frederick II (the Great) of Prussia, Maria Theresa and her son Joseph II of Austria, and Catherine the Great of Russia were able to create the appearance of enlightened reform, and even to effect some benefit, but these changes were carried out with little alteration of the existing political and social framework. The Austrian and Russian empires especially would remain hesitant toward change well into the next century. The later effects of this residual conservatism will become an integral part of our understanding of developments in eastern Europe down to the present day.

As viewed from the perspective of our own time, any of the attempts at reform in the eighteenth century would have side-effects, reactions. In reality the full impact of the Enlightenment was not felt until the end of the century. The effect of these ideas on the American Revolution could not be fully appreciated at that time. Equally, it should be noted that many of the events associated with the French Revolution (our next chapter) would cause a prolonged reaction to the rationalism of the Enlightenment.

IDENTIFICATIONS

Identify each one of the following as used in the text. Refer to the text as necessary.

	Text Page
Newtonian world view	416
tabula rasa	416
Denis Diderot	420
Cesare Beccaria	422
physiocrats	422
The Wealth of Nations	423
laissez-faire economics	423
The Spirit of the Laws	424
The Social Contract	424-425
Madame de Pompadour	426
Mary Wollstonecraft	428
robot	429
Josephinism	430
Peter III of Russia	432
Treaty of Kuchuk-Kainardji	433
partitions of Poland	433-435
Pugachev's Rebellion	436

MAP EXERCISE A

Draw the boundaries of 18th-century Prussia, Austria, Hungary and Russia in relationship to the changing boundaries of Poland. Circle cities/centers of Enlightenment thought throughout Europe.

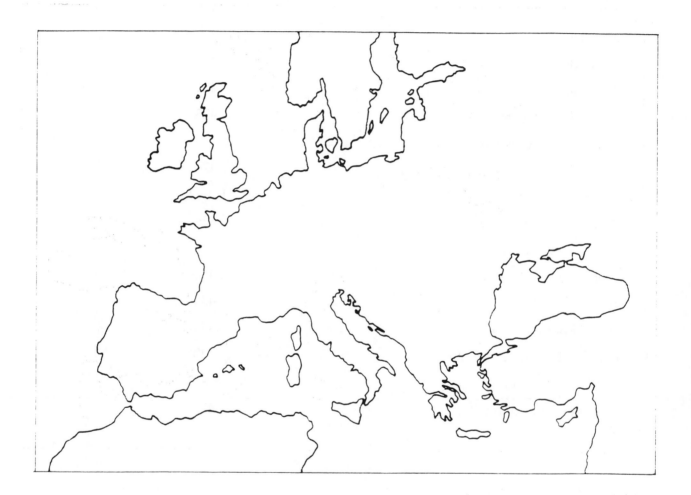

MAP EXERCISE B

Mark the current boundaries of Germany, Poland, the Czech Republic, Slovakia, Hungary, Bulgaria, Rumania, Belorussia, Ukraine and Russia. Compare with Exercise A.

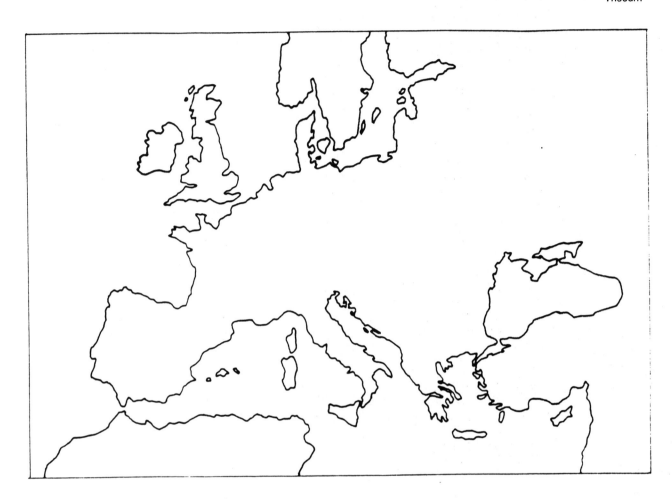

SHORT-ANSWER EXERCISES

Multiple-Choice

_____ 1. Which of the following is the least accurate statement about the *philosophes:* (a) they were most often men from the upper classes of society, (b) they held a common desire for reform of society, government, and thought, (c) they used the printed word as their major weapon, (d) they were not well organized and disagreed on many points.

_____ 2. Which of the following works was not written by Voltaire? (a) *Letters on the English* (b) *The Persian Letters* (c) *Elements of the Philosophy of Newton* (d) *Candide.*

_____ 3. Which is the most accurate statement about the churches of France during the Age of Enlightenment: (a) they provided justification for the status quo, (b) the upper classes dominated the upper clergy, (c) they owned a great deal of land, (d) all of these.

_____ 4. During this period it was argued that the purpose of laws was to achieve: (a) justice for all classes, (b) the greatest good for the greatest number, (c) religious toleration for all peoples, (d) none of these.

_____ 5. Adam Smith's philosophy of economics basically advocated all but: (a) increased tariff regulation, (b) free pursuit of economic self-interest, (c) exploitation of the earth's physical resources, (d) free trade.

_____ 6. The foundation of Montesquieu's ideas for reform stem from: (a) his study of sociology, (b) his effort to support aristocratic institutions, (c) the inefficient absolutism of monarchy in France, (d) his knowledge of the development of the English cabinet system.

_____ 7. Which of the following was not written by Rousseau: (a) *Nathan the Wise* (b) *The Social Contract* (c) *Discourse on the Moral Effects of the Arts and Sciences* (d) *Discourse on the Origin of Inequality.*

_____ 8. The concept that under certain circumstances some people must be forced to be free is associated with the thinking of: (a) Rousseau, (b) Montesquieu, (c) Bentham, (d) Locke.

_____ 9. In the last analysis the Enlightened Monarchs of the eighteenth century supported change and innovation because: (a) of potential benefits leading to greater international prestige, (b) it reduced their dependency on military strength, (c) a desire to impress their female subjects, (d) all of these.

_____ 10. Which of the following rulers is not normally associated with the ideas of Enlightened Absolutism? (a) Joseph II of Austria, (b) Catherine the Great of Russia, (c) George III of England, (d) Frederick II of Prussia.

True-False

_____ 1. A long-term effect of the Enlightenment has been the idea that change brings improvement within Western societies.

_____ 2. John Locke fully accepted the Christian view of humankind flawed by sin.

_____ 3. English societies of Freemasons were early advocates of reading and debate.

_____ 4. The Scottish *philosophe* David Hume's work challenging the idea of miracles was titled *Miracles of Miracles.*

_____ 5. Gotthold Lessing's *Nathan the Wise* actually called for the religious toleration of non-Christians.

_____ 6. François Quesnay headed a French mercantile association opposed to physiocratic thought.

_____ 7. Montesquieu's analysis of the separation of powers within the British constitutional system called attention to the role of patronage and corruption.

_____ 8. Rousseau's influence in Western thought ended with his death in 1778.

_____ 9. Mary Wollstonecraft argued that it was in a woman's best interest to be the sensual slave of man.

_____ 10. Leopold II, upon succession to the Austrian throne, made a concerted effort to repeal some, but not all of the reforms of his brother Joseph II.

Completion

1. In comparison to all others, _____ was the freest country of the eighteenth century.

2. _____ was the English journal which encouraged a wider discussion of eighteenth century ideas.

3. The publication of the _____ can be considered the greatest literary monument of the Enlightenment era.

4. The idea that was advanced in an attempt to establish a natural and rational base to religion was known as _____.

5. *The Decline and Fall of the Roman Empire* was written by _____.

6. The comment, "first servant of the State," is associated with _____.

7. The most coldly rational of the so-called Enlightened Absolutists was _____.

8. Catherine the Great was of _____ descent.

9. _____ was the title of a set of guidelines issued by Catherine the Great that reflected some of the political ideas of the Enlightenment.

10. During the second half of the eighteenth century the formal boundaries of _____ were removed from the map of Europe.

FOR FURTHER CONSIDERATION

1. Explain the concept of deism. How is deism a reflection of Enlightenment thought?

2. Discuss the thinking and work of Baron Montesquieu. In your opinion what has been the long-term impact of his work?

3. Discuss the thinking and works of Jean Jacques Rousseau. In your opinion what has been the long-term impact of his work?

4. What is meant by the term Enlightened Absolutism? How is it a reflection of eighteenth-century thought?

5. Generally, how would you describe the overall impact of Enlightenment ideas on Europe? Consider these ideas as reflected in our own society today.

ANSWERS

Multiple-Choice

		Text Page
1.	A	419
2.	B	419-420
3.	D	421
4.	B	422
5.	A	423
6.	C	424
7.	A	424
8.	A	425
9.	A	428
10.	C	429-431

True-False

1.	T	415
2.	F	416
3.	T	418
4.	F	422
5.	T	422
6.	F	423
7.	F	424
8.	F	425
9.	F	428
10.	T	431

Completion

1.	England	416
2.	*The Spectator*	418
3.	*Encyclopedia*	420
4.	deism	421
5.	Edward Gibbon	422
6.	Frederick the Great	429
7.	Joseph II of Austria	429
8.	German	432
9.	*Instructions*	433
10.	Poland	434-435

◆ ◆ ◆ ◆ ◆ ◆ ◆

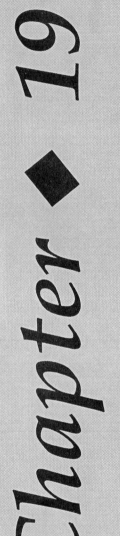

Chapter ◆ 19

THE FRENCH REVOLUTION

COMMENTARY

As a major turning point in human history the French Revolution represents a culmination of eighteenth-century ideas, economic transitions, and subtle transformations within the European social structure. It was directly coupled to the obvious abuses of what we now call the old regime. As a turning point, developments in France that actually began in 1788 cannot be ignored. For these events, personalities, crises, considerable violence, and much confusion set in motion forces that have ever since affected the social and political foundation of the entire world.

Under the old regime the ruling classes had assumed for centuries that things would always be as they had been. Whether in the realm of aristocratic privilege or within the exclusive prerogatives of the Catholic Church there appeared little desire or need for new approaches to the difficulties of human life. Change, what there was of it, was meant to be slow, remaining imperceptible from one generation to the next. But the influence of Enlightenment thinking, the development of modern capitalism, and the related growth of cities were all motivating forces for the upheaval.

France as the center of European intellectual life was ripe for change, and as unresolved economic problems lingered unattended for decades, revolution came in the late 1780s. The nature of the French Revolution, however, was not immediately radical, or immediately a revolution of the masses as it is often perceived. For years a relatively small group of men, largely professional and with some propertied wealth, attempted to steer a moderate course. Faced with aristocratic obstinacy and monarchial inconsistency, these men were at the same time effectively ruling France and working to adopt the principle of limited monarchy. Their efforts failed and the revolution was soon radicalized. Before 1792, however, the legislative efforts at reform, although not wholly adopted, were impressive. Such statements as the Declaration of the Rights of Man and the Civil Constitution of the Clergy were not only signs of eighteenth-century thought but had the further effect of opening the floodgates of reform in the next century.

What brought on the revolution was the French financial crisis of the 1780s. This was the result of economic problems reaching back half a century. France's losses to England in the Seven Years' War, coupled with the related support of the American colonies during their revolution, were notable factors. Poor harvests, inequitable taxes, monarchial extravagance, all combined to encourage Louis XVI's original decision to convene the Estates-General. From that fateful decision can be traced the development of the Revolution in France. The tug-of-war that followed led the French people into a state of political, social, economic, and religious turmoil that ended with the birth of the modern era. First, the moderates of the National Constituent Assembly attempted a platform of moderate reform within a constitutional monarchy. The program presented was never genuinely endorsed by the king, and other groups, largely urban and lower on the socioeconomic ladder, the *sansculottes,* were increasingly involved. The character of the Revolution changed as foreign invaders, hoping to salvage the throne of Louis XVI, pressed into France. Forced between increasingly radical change and foreign domination, the people of France chose the former, thereby saving the Revolution from extinction and giving birth to today's concept of nationalism. By 1793, and along with the Jacobin excesses under Robespierre, the republic was created. France would never again remain long under monarchy. Yet the Reign of Terror fostered a reaction that for a time stabilized the tumult of the revolution in France. Although still another government followed as the Directory (Constitution of 1795), it remained to be seen whether this government could do what several preceding ones had failed to do—namely, consolidate the many changes, in reality several centuries' worth, that had been produced by revolution within only a few years.

IDENTIFICATIONS

Identify each one of the following as used in the text. Refer to the text as necessary.

	Text Page
parlements	440
Jacques Necker	440
cahiers de doléances	444
Tennis Court Oath	444
August 4, 1789	446
Olympe de Gouges	448
Chapelier Law	448
assignats	450
émigrés	450
sans-culottes	454
leveé en masse	457
Society of Revolutionary Republican Women	457-458
dechristianization of France	458
Reign of Terror	458-460
enragés	459
Law of 22 Prairial	459
Gracchus Babeuf	461

MAP EXERCISE A

Locate each of the following on the accompanying map:

1. English Channel
2. Bay of Biscay
3. Mediterranean Sea
4. Cities of Metz, Lyons, Marseilles, Toulon, Paris, Verdun
5. Provinces of Burgundy and Brittany
6. Departments of Vendée and Gironde

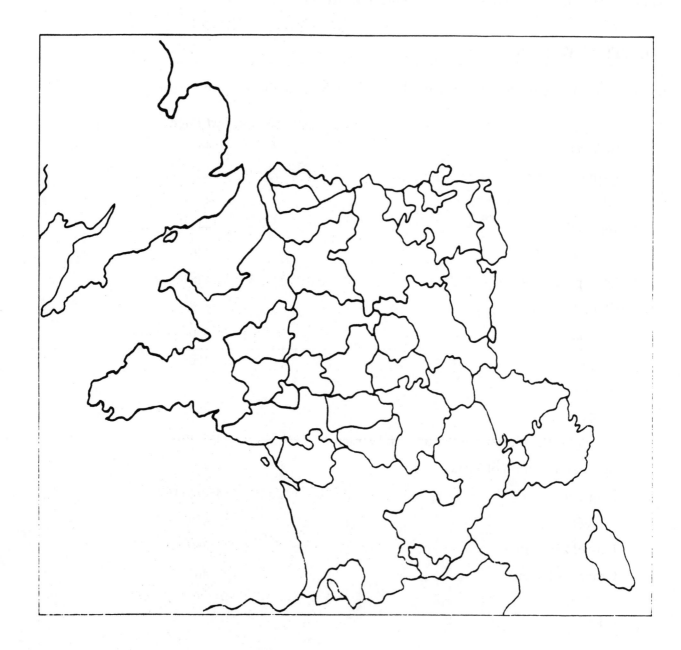

MAP EXERCISE B

In the space below draw a free-hand map of modern France. Include at least **three** rivers, two mountain ranges, the capital city and all the countries that touch the borders of France. Don't forget Andorra.

SHORT-ANSWER EXERCISES

Multiple-Choice

_____ 1. The text notes that the French Revolution was caused by the fact that France: (a) gained new colonial territories as a result of her support of the American Revolution, (b) was a rich nation with an impoverished government, (c) was in debt way out of proportion when compared with other European states, (d) all of these.

_____ 2. The budget presented by: (a) Étienne Charles Loménie de Brienne, (b) René Maupeou, (c) Jacques Necker, (d) Charles Alexandre de Calonne, did the most to excite opposition against the aristocracy and the government.

_____ 3. What is often considered as the document that put an end to the old regime in France was: (a) the *cahiers*, (b) The Civil Constitution of the Clergy, (c) The Declaration of the Rights of Man and Citizen, (d) The Tennis Court Oath.

_____ 4. After the passage of the Civil Constitution of the Clergy, the Catholic Church in France was: (a) increasingly supportive, (b) decreasingly supportive, (c) openly opposed, (d) none of these, to the French Revolution.

_____ 5. The 1793 revolt in western France was in support of the: (a) Jacobins, (b) Prussians, (c) monarchy, (d) Girondists.

_____ 6. In 1793 the Cathedral of Notre Dame became the: (a) headquarters of the Jacobin party, (b) Temple of Virtue, (c) prison of Marie Antoinette, (d) Temple of Reason.

_____ 7. The approximately 25,000 victims of the Reign of Terror were largely: (a) lower class, (b) clergy, (c) aristocracy, (d) none of these.

_____ 8. By the end of 1795 legislation in France regarding the status of women: (a) liberalized divorce procedures for them, (b) supported their involvement in the political process, (c) upgraded their status in the eyes of the Church, (d) left them with somewhat less freedom than enjoyed before 1789.

_____ 9. The Thermidorean Constitution of the Year III (1795) required that members of the legislature be: (a) married, (b) widowed, (c) female, (d) actually none of these choices is wholly accurate.

_____ 10. In the latter half of the 1790s the government of the Directory was primarily supported by: (a) *sans-culottes* groups, (b) the army, (c) the Catholic Church, (d) Napoleon Bonaparte.

True-False

_____ 1. Their were no casualties in the events surrounding the fall of the Bastille.

_____ 2. The "Great Fear" occurred in the summer of 1789 as a result of rumors of coming food shortages.

_____ 3. One of the major reasons for not immediately repudiating the French national debt was that much of it was owed to the very people represented by the Third Estate.

_____ 4. The new currency issued by the National Assembly near the end of 1790 was backed by lands confiscated from the aristocracy of France.

_____ 5. The 1792 massacre of persons in Paris jails came to be known as the "October Days."

_____ 6. An example of the effect the French Revolution was having on other European states was the burning of Voltaire's works by Catherine the Great.

_____ 7. Lazare Carnot, a prominent Jacobin, was responsible for the organization of republican military armies.

_____ 8. The so-called *enragés* were a radical group of *sans-culottes* that urged greater price regulations and a more extreme policy of dechristianization.

_____ 9. The Thermidorean Reaction was chiefly supported by the aristocracy in combination with the *sans-culottes*.

_____ 10. One of the unanticipated results of the Thermidorean Reaction was a notable revival of Catholicism.

Completion

1. In 1774 _____ became the king of France.

2. The question of _____ procedures remained an unresolved problem in 1788 and during the earliest meetings of the Estates General.

3. The taking of the Bastille resulted in the release of _____ prisoners.

4. The 1791 Declaration of _____ was an effort by the kings of Austria and Prussia to protect the French royal family.

5. The most advanced and best organized political group of the National Constituent Assembly was the _____.

6. The French Convention of 1792 actually took its name from the _____ of 1787.

7. The battle of _____ in 1792 is often considered as the victory of democracy over aristocracy.

8. _____ took a position against the French Revolution in his work titled *Reflections on the Revolution in France.*

9. The more extreme aspect of the Thermidorean Reaction is known as the _____.

10. The 1795 riots against the Convention brought attention to _____.

FOR FURTHER CONSIDERATION

1. Discuss the financial crisis in France on the eve of the French Revolution. Why was the problem so grave in a country that had considerable wealth? Distinguish between the rural and urban aspects of the problem.

2. What were the policies of the National Constituent Assembly toward the Catholic Church? How would these policies "revolutionize" church-state relations throughout Europe?

3. What caused the Reign of Terror in France? Are events such as this normal in revolutionary movements? Was there a similar or comparable situation in the American Revolution?

4. Describe the Thermidorean Reaction. Why should these events be considered as important parts of the era of the French Revolution?

5. The French Revolution is often characterized as the beginning of the end of the old regime in Europe as well as a sign of things to come in the nineteenth and twentieth centuries. Comment on this statement using appropriate examples as necessary.

Answers

Multiple-Choice

		Text Page
1.	B	440
2.	C	440
3.	C	446
4.	C	450
5.	C	455
6.	D	458
7.	A	460
8.	D	460-461
9.	D	461
10.	B	462

True-False

1.	F	445
2.	F	445
3.	T	450
4.	F	450
5.	F	452
6.	T	456
7.	T	457
8.	T	459
9.	F	460
10.	T	460

Completion

1.	Louis XVI	440
2.	voting/representation	444
3.	seven	445
4.	Pillnitz	451
5.	Jacobins	451-452
6.	American Constitutional Convention	453
7.	Valmy	453
8.	Edmund Burke	455
9.	White Terror	460
10.	Napoleon Bonaparte	461

THE AGE OF NAPOLEON AND THE TRIUMPH OF ROMANTICISM

COMMENTARY

The years of confusion created by the revolution in France set the stage for Napoleon Bonaparte's control of that state. His impact on French and European life was such that it is almost impossible to read through this era without acknowledging the Napoleonic legacy. Napoleon was more than a legend. He was for an entire European generation the dominant factor of life and politics. Although the era passed it most certainly established the grounds for the legend. Bonaparte's accession is as much a product of his country's past as it was a sign of what future generations would inevitably face.

The Consulate and Empire years were the achievements of a skilled and ruthless premodern dictator. It was Napoleon's flair coupled with many years of success that helped create the legend. He was, at the same time, a product of the Revolution in France and of Romanticism in Europe. His ambition was his undoing. For over a decade Napoleon and the armed forces he led dominated most of Europe and thereby unleashed a chain of forces that have affected conditions to the present day. Most important, it is nationalism that emerges in modern form during this period. And it was nationalism that helped sustain Napoleon's control over France and Europe.

Exposed to both liberalism and nationalism, people in the areas ruled by Napoleon were taken with Enlightenment principles and French revolutionary ideals. The past had been abolished, Europe was dominated by the French, and the future was uncertain. Increasingly French controls were felt to be burdensome, and this fact soon led to opposition and revolt against Napoleon's rule in Europe. Prussia's defeat by France at Jena had quick and long-lasting effects, which in turn would solidify the German people as never before. The reforms within Prussian society and in the military not only strengthened Prussia's resistance to France but were eventually instrumental in Napoleon's defeat.

Popular resistance to Napoleon's rule in Spain would soon cripple French effectiveness there and drain overall resources. Yet Austrian restlessness led to another Napoleonic victory at Wagram in 1809 and thereby to his marriage to the daughter of the Austrian emperor.

By 1810 Napoleon's rule was at the edge of a general European challenge led by Russia. To offset this threat the Emperor made the fateful decision to invade Russia. This campaign ultimately led to the showdown between France and the other great powers of Europe. The campaign reached its climax in September 1812. At the great Battle of Borodino, east of Moscow, nearly 100,000 casualties were experienced, and though French armies soon entered Moscow they were also soon forced to retreat. This retreat, coupled with Russian destruction of the countryside, was the beginning of the end for Napoleon and full of lessons for future generals to ponder. The failure of Napoleon in Russia aroused opposition throughout Europe and within two years he was forced into exile on Elba, a small island off the west coast of Italy; and not far from his Corsican birthplace.

Having finally defeated Napoleon, representatives of the victorious European powers and of the restored monarchy in France met in the Austrian capital of Vienna in the hope of restoring stability to the continent. The views expressed there were largely those of the old regime. The old regime had been the symbol of aristocratic rule and social stability before and it was anticipated to be so again. What few recognized at the time were the vast undercurrents of change loosed by the French Revolution, coupled to the growth of industrialization, and now fostered by the growth of liberalism and nationalism, the "isms" destined to dominate the century. With Napoleon "safely" on Elba the authors of the Vienna settlement attempted to replace Napoleonic Europe with a Europe most representative of the previous century. At the same time each attempted to assert his own national ambitions. The territorial settlements and restorations reflected these ambitions and were to become the source of future problems. In the sense of primary objectives, the Congress was a success. Thanks to Wellington and Blucher, the coalition survived Napoleon's brief return to the continent. Yet no settlement, particularly one cast so soon after hostilities ended, could have been a complete success. Too much had happened in the previous twenty-five years. At the same time the Congress of Vienna did establish a period of relative calm in Europe—a calm not entirely broken until the outbreak of World War I.

One of the clearest signs of fundamental change during this era is the advent of the intellectual movement called Romanticism. "In many ways it was a hostile response to the Enlightenment" (text p. 478). Throughout Europe intellectual manifestation of this reaction can be noted. The new emphasis on nature and individualism was a deep reflection of a new European era. The arts as well as religion were tremendously stimulated by this Romantic protest against the rationalism of the Enlightenment. The new stress on the individual, on history, on a nation's past, made Romanticism an important adjunct to the idea of liberalism and nationalism. Hence, Romanticism and the other events of this period all are combined in an important historical shift within the Western heritage.

IDENTIFICATIONS

Identify each one of the following as used in the text. Refer to the text as necessary.

	Text Page
Horatio Nelson	466 and 469
Abbé Siéyès	467
Consulate government	467-468
Treaty of Amiens	467 and 469
Organic Articles of 1802	468
Continental System	470
General Kutuzov	473
Battle of Borodino	473
Treaty of Chaumont	475
The Hundred Days	476
Holy Alliance	478
Quadruple Alliance	478
Romantics	478
Émile	479
"categorical imperative"	480
Methodism	483
The Genius of Christianity	483
thesis, antithesis, synthesis	484

MAP EXERCISE A

Locate each of the following on the accompanying map:

1.	Corsica	6.	Marseilles
2.	Brittany (France)	7.	Berlin
3.	Nieman River	8.	Vienna
4.	Island of Elba	9.	Warsaw
5.	Paris	10.	Moscow

Locate each of these battles:

1.	Trafalgar	6.	Borodino
2.	Austerlitz	7.	Dresden
3.	Jena	8.	Leipzig
4.	Friedland	9.	Waterloo
5.	Wagram		

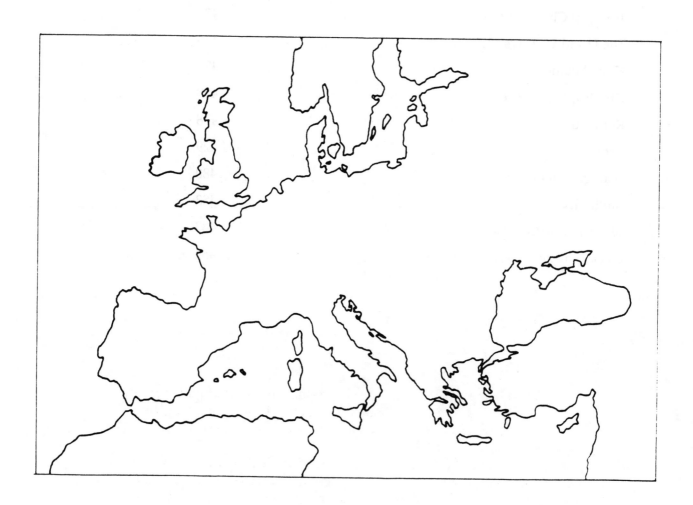

MAP EXERCISE B

Outline the borders of the modern states of Europe. Mark the extent of the French Imperium as it appeared in 1812.

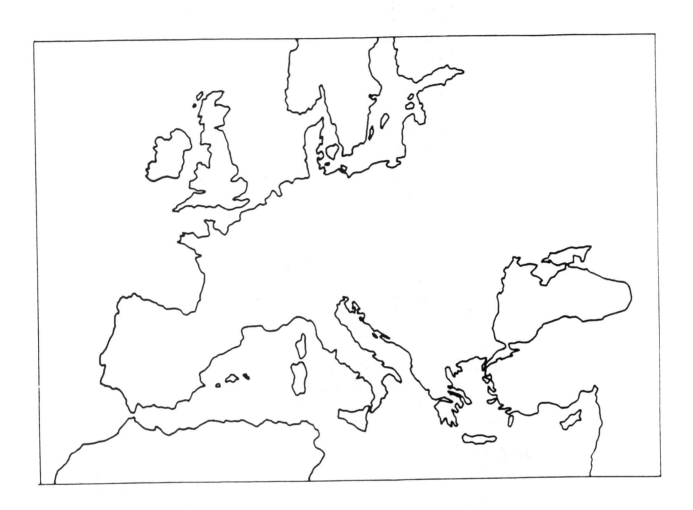

SHORT-ANSWER EXERCISES

Multiple-Choice

_____ 1. The Napoleonic Constitution of 1799: (a) was outwardly dictatorial, (b) was modeled after that of the United States, (c) contained a suggestion of democratic principles and republican theories, (d) was none of these.

_____ 2. With the Napoleonic Code of 1804: (a) fathers had extensive control over their families, (b) females could now receive inheritances, (c) labor unions were forbidden, (d) all of these were part of the Code.

_____ 3. One of the reasons Napoleon established the Bonapartist dynasty in 1804 was: (a) the need to publicly demonstrate supremacy over the Church in France, (b) the need to demonstrate supremacy over the Pope, (c) that it would create a recognizable heir to his throne, (d) he believed it was necessary for him to get into a good college.

_____ 4. The Continental System: (a) was an effective weapon against British trade, (b) encouraged smuggling, (c) prevented smuggling, (d) created a free trade zone throughout Europe.

_____ 5. Which of the following would not be associated with the reforms of the Napoleonic Code as it effected France and much of Europe: (a) Roman Catholic Church's monopoly on religion ended, (b) feudal obligations of the peasants disappeared, (c) class distinctions were re-inforced, (d) the reforming ideas of the Enlightenment began to reach much of Europe.

_____ 6. Rebellion against French rule in Spain came from the: (a) nobility and upper clergy, (b) peasants and monastic leaders, (c) upper classes, (d) peasants and the lower clergy.

_____ 7. Which of the following was never married to Napoleon Bonaparte: (a) Marie Louise, (b) Gretchen de Faust, (c) Josephine de Beauharnais, (d) the daughter of Austria's monarch.

_____ 8. Napoleon's final exile was to the island of: (a) St. Helena, (b) Corsica, (c) Elba, (d) Sardinia.

_____ 9. Friedrich Schlegel's _Lucinde_ (1799) shocked many contemporaries because: (a) it openly discussed sexual activity, (b) it showed a woman in equal status to a man, (c) it did not cater to existing prejudices against women, (d) of all of these.

_____ 10. The idea that religion is a great and emotional experience would be least associated with: (a) Immanuel Kant, (b) Friedrich Schleiermacher, (c) John Wesley, (d) François René de Chateaubriand.

True-False

_____ 1. With the complete support of the government at Paris, Napoleon negotiated the Treaty of Campo Formio (October 1797) which took the Austrian Empire out of the First Coalition.

_____ 2. In 1804, though overwhelmingly supported by the people of France, Napoleon still insisted on placing the imperial crown on his own head.

_____ 3. The Treaty of Tilsit between Russia's Tzar Alexander and Napoleon Bonaparte cost Prussia dearly.

_____ 4. The German political leaders von Stein and von Hardenburg generally supported democratic reform in Prussia.

_____ 5. Sir Arthur Wellesley commanded British forces during the Peninsular War in Spain.

_____ 6. The Grand Army of Napoleon which invaded Russia in 1812 was composed of about 160,000 soldiers.

_____ 7. Napoleon was defeated by the combined armies of the other European states in 1813 at Leipzig.

_____ 8. In *Émile* Rousseau urged the importance of strict upbringing of children that they might later flourish as adults.

_____ 9. In his *The Genius of Christianity* François Chateaubriand described his conversion from Judaism to Methodism.

_____ 10. Johann Gottfried Herder stressed the acceptability of universal culture and the common humanity of the entire planet.

Completion

1. After Napoleon's defeat of the Austrians in October 1797, France's only real enemy was _____.

2. The execution of the _____ put an end to royalist plots against Napoleon's government.

3. Probably the battle at _____ against the combined forces of Russia and Austria was Napoleon's greatest victory.

4. One of the outcomes of the 1809 French victory at Wagram was Napoleon's marriage to _____.

5. _____ was the French representative to the Congress of Vienna.

6. *The Prelude* was written by _____ .

7. The most rebellious of the Romantic writers was _____.

8. _____ is the story of a man, who, weary of life, made a pact with the devil.

9. _____ argued that particularly strong rulers can impose their will on others.

10. _____ was the most important historical writer of the entire Romantic era.

FOR FURTHER CONSIDERATION

1. Explain the rise of Napoleon Bonaparte. Can this be considered a classic example of man making history, or were conditions favorable to the emergence of a "Napoleon-like" leader?

2. How did France under Napoleon actually control Europe? Was there a common theme to all of Napoleon's actions during this era? Why were the European states for so long unable to organize against the French threat?

3. Discuss the circumstances that brought about the Congress of Vienna. What were the major successes and failures of the meeting? Are there any long-term, historical factors to be associated with the Congress of Vienna? If so, what are they?

4. Define Romanticism. What do you see as the overall impact of this concept on Western civilization?

5. Why does Romanticism impact upon religion? Are their "romantic" aspects to modern religious practices; if so, what are they? State your position in detail.

ANSWERS

Multiple-Choice

		Text Page
1.	C	467
2.	D	468
3.	C	469
4.	B	470
5.	C	471
6.	D	472
7.	B	*passim*
8.	A	476
9.	D	482
10.	A	483

True-False

1.	F	466
2.	T	469
3.	T	470
4.	F	471
5.	T	472
6.	F	473
7.	T	475
8.	F	479
9.	F	483
10.	F	483

Completion

1.	Great Britain	466
2.	Duke of Enghien	468
3.	Austerlitz	470
4.	Austrian Archduchess Marie Louise	472
5.	Talleyrand	476
6.	William Wordsworth	481
7.	Lord Byron	481
8.	Faust	482
9.	J.G. Fichte	483
10.	Georg W. F. Hegel	484

For Further Consideration of the Documents

Each of the following questions is designed to help you reach a better understanding of certain of the original documents presented in the last five chapters of the text. Feel free to use the page numbers provided to refer back to the document as necessary. The value of a primary historical source should not be underestimated; it helps us understand the nature of the era in which it was written.

Wakefield Demands More Occupations for Women (p. 376-377)
1. Using contemporary terms and examples express the ideas and inequalities presented here in your own words.

The Atlantic Passage (pp. 402-403)
2. What does Captain Phillips mean by "after all our expectations to be defeated by their mortality?" What are your views on black-white relations since colonial times? What in your opinion is the current status of race relations in America? In the world?

Rousseau on Men and Women (pp. 426-427)
3. In this regard list the areas of Rousseau's thought that you agree with? That you disagree with?

The Sans-Culotte (p. 453)
4. Who would be considered the equivalent persons in our society today? Compare and contrast them with the *sans-culotte* of eighteenth-century France.

Chateaubriand Describes a Gothic Church (pp. 484-485)
5. Is this an accurate reflection of the Middle Ages? Explain your answer fully.

Chapter 21

RESTORATION, REACTION, AND REFORM (1815-1832)

COMMENTARY

Any student taking a serious look at the nineteenth century must define and study the mainstream "isms" associated with that era of change. A working knowledge of nationalism, liberalism, republicanism, socialism, communism and conservatism is basic to an understanding of the last century of Western history. Pay close attention to nationalism for it remains among the most moving of the "isms" and is re-appearing in a virulent form in several world trouble spots today.

The restored order brought on by the Vienna settlement at the conclusion of the Napoleonic Wars was intended more to bring stability to the European state system than to make any accommodation with the forces unleashed by the French Revolution. In the aftermath of these wars the conservative leadership of Europe sought a guarantee that emerging concepts of liberalism would remain mere ideas. Yet each country was faced with political groups converted to the liberal faith and anxious for change. Confronted with demands for social and political reform after 1815, most leaders attempted to reinstitute conservative or traditional means of governmental control. The approach was different in each country, but the goal of order and stability remained the same. In those places where even comparatively mild reforms were considered, short-lived experiments with political, economic, and social reforms languished. At the same time it was clear that the social-political fabric of Europe had been altered by the French Revolution and the emerging patterns of industrialization. Throughout the remainder of the nineteenth century the ideas associated with liberalism, nationalism, and soon, socialism, would continually play a vital role.

Even before 1820 there were a number of serious outcroppings of liberal fervor, and the responses of the governments throughout the continent provide examples of several historical forces at work. Note that university students increasingly were supportive of liberal and nationalist goals.

While Austria would continue to dominate the peoples of central Europe several nationalist problems smoldered beneath the surface of reaction. German students, Hungarian Magyars, and an increasingly active political middle class each saw potential advantages in liberal and national reform. Austria's Metternich skillfully handled these forces until near the mid-century point and thereby gave the appearance of conservative order.

Popular unrest occurred in orderly Britain as radical leaders stirred the discontented. The "Peterloo" affair, or massacre, is a symptom of the trouble there. At the same time ultraroyalism prevailed in France during the early decades of the post-Napoleonic era.

More interestingly from today's perspective are the events on the South American continent and in Mexico in the first quarter of the nineteenth century. Napoleon's wars had been disruptive in Europe for nearly twenty years and had effectively loosened centuries-old imperial control in South America. Led by Creole elites throughout the region whole sections of the former Iberian (Spain and Portugal) empires moved toward independence in a manner not unlike the former British thirteen colonies in the previous century. Under the leadership of men like José de San Martin, Bernardo O'Higgins, and Simón Bolívar independent states emerged in South America. Fathers Hildalgo and Morelos stirred Mexico toward independence at the same time. The reforms brought forth, however had only a marginal effect on the lower classes of the region.

In Eastern Europe nationalist movements in Greece and Serbia during this era should also be noted. In Russia the Decembrist revolt of 1825 was commonly viewed as one such outcropping. Yet it was an unsuccessful revolt, which was ruthlessly crushed by Czar Nicholas I, Alexander I's younger brother. The establishment of the independence of Greece and Belgium were examples, though minor ones, of successful liberal and nationalist revolts. In these cases, however, it should be noted that both were successful only because conservative states and international considerations combined to give aid and comfort to the revolutionaries.

The Revolution of 1830 in France, although moderately liberal in tone, did not truly satisfy the demands of most reformers. Louis Philippe's government attempted, and by 1848, had failed to establish broad enough liberal support among the politicians and people of France. Hence, eighteen years after Charles X went into exile he was followed by the "King of the French." In England parliamentary compromise and political accommodation in regard to Catholic emancipation temporarily resolved the Irish Question. But passage of the Great Reform Bill of 1832 only whetted the liberal appetite for further reforms.

As the midcentury approached it was clear that the reform efforts of the liberals had been only moderately successful and only in some countries. Change had taken place but had been, on occasion, coupled with serious violence. Liberals looked to the future for increased support from within the growing middle classes and toward corresponding political, social, and economic gains.

Identifications

Identify each one of the following as used in the text. Refer to the text as necessary.

	Text Page
the German Confederation	493
"War of Liberation"	493
tercentenary of the Ninety-five theses	493
Karl Sand	493-494
Carlsbad Decrees	494
Combination Acts of 1799	494
"Peterloo" Massacre	494-495
ultraroyalism	495
Quadruple Alliance	496
George Canning	497
Philhellenic societies	497
Karageorge	498
Toussaint L'Ouverture	498 and 500
Creole elites	500
José María Morelos y Pavón	502
Dom Pedro	502
Decembrist Revolt	504
Organic Statute	504
Charles X	505
Prince de Polignac	505
July Monarchy	506
Lord Palmerston	507
Convention of 1839	507
Daniel O'Connell	508

MAP EXERCISE A

On the accompanying map outline the early eighteenth-century boundaries of Mexico and the states of Central and South America.

MAP EXERCISE B

Locate each of the following on this map of the Caribbean Basin.

Florida	Puerto Rico
Bahamas	Panama
Cuba	Venezuela
Island of Hispaniola	Mexico
Haiti	Barbados
Jamaica	Curaçao

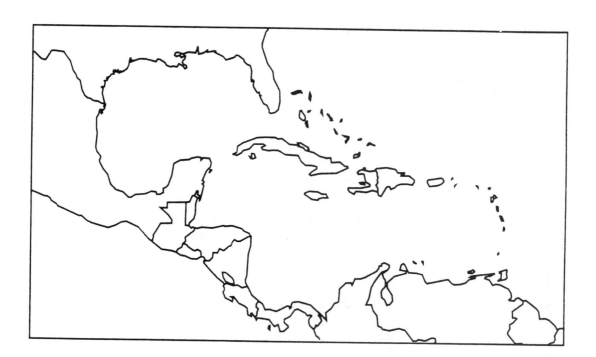

SHORT-ANSWER EXERCISES

Multiple-Choice

_____ 1.   The real goal of this era's political liberals was: (a) mass democracy, (b) political reforms and greater representation based on property ownership, (c) free education for all, (d) the end of poverty.

_____ 2.   (a) Economic Liberalism, (b) Nationalism, (c) Christianity, (d) Urbanization, was an important complement to liberalism in this period.

_____ 3.   Which of the following occurred in England: (a) passage of the Carlsbad Decrees, (b) murder of the Duke of Berri, (c) announcement of the Protocol of Troppau, (d) clash between troops and reformers at St. Peter's Fields.

_____ 4. Alexander I's reign (1801-1825) can be considered as: (a) liberal throughout, (b) conservative throughout, (c) initially liberal and later conservative, (d) none of these.

_____ 5. The Concert of Europe was: (a) a radical political party, (b) the dream child of the Russian Tsar, (c) a symphony orchestra, (d) none of these.

_____ 6. European interest in the Ottoman Empire stemmed from: (a) the desire for commercial access, (b) direct competition between Austria and Russia, (c) a desire to have access to the shrines in the Holy Land, (d) all of these factors.

_____ 7. Early in the nineteenth century: (a) Austria, (b) England, (c) France, (d) Russia, assumed the role as a protector of Serbia.

_____ 8. The Decembrist movement in Russia wanted to achieve all of the following except: (a) constitutional government, (b) election of Tsars, (c) Constantine to be Tsar, (d) reforms.

_____ 9. The Four Ordinances issued by Charles X: (a) restricted freedom of the press, (b) restricted the franchise to only the wealthiest people in the country, (c) brought a strong reaction throughout much of French society, (d) all of these.

_____ 10. The Great Reform Bill of 1832 finally passed because: (a) of fears of mob violence, (b) new elections were held for the House of Commons, (c) the king threatened to alter the structure of the House of Lords, (d) of the Peterloo Massacre.

True-False

_____ 1. Among the great age of "isms" nationalism is considered the most powerful.

_____ 2. The Combination Acts were passed as a result of a December 1811 mass protest near London at Spa Fields.

_____ 3. An important factor in repressive measures taken by Louis XVIII of France can be found in the 1820 murder of the Duke de Berri.

_____ 4. Without question, Tsar Alexander I of Russia is considered the chief architect of the post-Vienna world.

_____ 5. Creole leaders in Latin America could be said to have developed a reform program based upon Enlightenment ideas and those associated with the American Revolution.

_____ 6. Mexico was the first area within Latin America to rise in revolution against Spain.

_____ 7. The revolt led by the Creole priest Hidalgo y Costilla was basically conservative in nature.

_____ 8. By the declaration of Nicholas I's Organic Statute Poland became an integral part of the Russian empire.

_____ 9. The so-called July Monarchy was headed by Louis Philippe as King of the French.

_____ 10. In 1832 England's Great Reform Bill extended the electoral franchise to all males over the age of twenty-one.

Completion

1. It is clear today that a common _____ is required as a basic block for the establishment of a new nation.

2. Many of the ideas of nineteenth-century liberals can be attributed to the writers of the _____.

3. During this period German student associations were called _____.

4. _____ was the first king of France after the abdication of Napoleon.

5. The document which declared that stable governments could intervene in other countries troubled by revolution and disorder was the _____.

6. Although established as a dictator, the hero of Chilean independence was _____.

7. The French city of _____ witnessed more than one serious workers' strike during the 1830s.

8. The first king of an independent Belgium was _____.

9. One of the most important articles of international relations until World War I had to do with the neutrality of _____.

10. The 1829 _____ Act passed by the British Parliament was directly related to the Irish Question.

FOR FURTHER CONSIDERATION

1. What was it about the nature of German society that made the plight of liberals there different? Can you envision what the future direction of German liberalism would be later in the nineteenth century?

2. Why is the movement for independence in Haiti viewed as the exception when compared with similar revolts throughout Latin America in this era? Has this altered Haiti's development into our time. Comment on recent Haitian troubles in this regard.

3. In regard to the revolutionary movements in Latin America during this period review the motives and role played by Creole elites. Compare their position with that of the European liberal movements at that time. Support your answer fully.

4. Throughout the nineteenth century, Russia was considered as the most conservative, least reform-minded, anti-liberal state. In your opinion what were the major reasons for this position?

5. What factors allowed Britain to be viewed as the most prominent testing place for European liberal thought?

ANSWERS

Multiple-Choice

		Text Page
1.	B	491
2.	A	491
3.	A	494
4.	C	496
5.	D	496-497
6.	D	498
7.	D	498
8.	B	503
9.	D	505
10.	C	508

True-False

1.	T	488
2.	F	494
3.	T	495
4.	F	496
5.	T	500
6.	F	501
7.	F	502
8.	T	504
9.	T	506
10.	F	508

Completion

1.	language	488-489
2.	Enlightenment	490
3.	*Burchenschaften*	493
4.	Louis XVIII	495
5.	Protocol of Troppau	497
6.	Bernardo O'Higgins	501
7.	Lyons	506-507
8.	Leopold of Saxe-Coburg	507
9.	Belgium	507
10.	Catholic Emancipation	508

◆ ◆ ◆ ◆ ◆ ◆ ◆

ECONOMIC ADVANCE AND SOCIAL UNREST (1830-1850)

COMMENTARY

Although the nascent industrialization of Europe occurred in the eighteenth century it was not until the close of the Napoleonic era that its effects were fully manifested. During the first fifty years of the nineteenth century, industrialization swept across Europe west to east, from England to eastern Europe. Destined to transform all European life, industrialization created many new uncertainties and fears for all classes. And yet the financial success experienced by the few acted as a continuing stimulant to the many. As a result of technological advance, the Europeans would come in large part to rule the world even into our own century; but for the nineteenth century the basic problems, economic, social, and political, resulting from industrial development had first to be understood. In this crucial period of European history all modes of human existence previously experienced would undergo a transformation not fully understood even today.

The nature of the factory system coupled with the ever-expanding railroad networks nurtured a wholly new social existence. Rapid urbanization outstripped any planning that might have alleviated its damaging effects. Rich and poor, high- and low-born, professional and laborer, were swept into the new vortex of industrialization. The process witnessed earliest in Great Britain recurred continuingly on the European continent. The middle classes were not only major contributors to the industrial revolution; they were its prime beneficiaries. Despite the obvious abuses illustrated in countless volumes of social criticism, the process, however harsh, continued unabated. The European labor force was drawn to urban factories by a mixture of desperate need, helplessness, and curiosity.

Correspondingly, as once rural peoples migrated to urban industrial environments they were exposed to the new modes of production. These factory-associated methods cheapened the labor value of workers and artisans alike through the process of *proletarianization*. These changes in work methods began to affect the traditional family structure, altering the position of children and ushering in more clearly defined gender dominated roles for women. Industrialization, and the resulting urbanization, coupled with Enlightenment ideas brought the problems of urban crime and the need for prison reform into focus. It is in this era that municipal police forces began to take on their modern appearance. These early police groups had the task of protecting property and persons as well as generally containing the less savory aspects of urban crime.

The classical economists, taking their lead from Adam Smith's work, sought to explain the phenomena of industrialization in terms of natural, and therefore unalterable, processes. Utopian socialists called for varying degrees of governmental intervention or encouraged the establishment of separate communal-like societies. Some groups, such as the Chartists, called for moderate reform through already existing political systems.

Chapter 22

Each group offered its position as the solution and each contributed to the thinking associated with socialism and ultimately Marxism.

In Marx's lifetime, his ideas of proletarian triumph, a classless society, and a better future were concepts that floated among many socialist theories of the mid-nineteenth century. Only the apparent success of so-called Marxist revolutions in the twentieth century has made Marxism the appealing force that it has been. Like many of his radical contemporaries, Marx attacked the government and industrial leadership for their contentment with the *status-quo* and for profit-taking at the expense, in his view, of the masses. Unlike others, Marx could not envision that capitalism would change by itself and, at least, partially remedy many of the abuses he decried.

By the middle of the century, concepts of liberalism, socialism, and nationalism were being widely discussed among intellectuals and students. The growing middle classes of Europe were achieving a social and political status undreamed of a half-century earlier. By 1848 new demands had been made on behalf of both the middle and working classes, and a series of revolutions swept the continent in that year.

Along with the overall and immediate factors associated with the causes of the revolutions of 1848, it should be understood that they had a far-reaching effect upon European history. In some ways the revolutions of 1848 are seen as a culmination of the revolutionary ideas associated with the French Revolution. Considered continent-wide, the general demands made for social and political justice and for national consolidation are true signs of modernity. The revolutions were the result of many developments in European life since the settlement at Vienna in 1815. They were as much the product of middle-class liberalism as they were of working-class demands. The two classes were, for a time, brought together by their respective economic aspirations and a vaguely defined hope for a better future regardless of class designation. In Italy, and largely throughout eastern Europe, with the notable exception of Russia, demands were voiced for national reorganization based not on a ruling dynasty but rather on the basis of a yet-undefined concept of the nation-state.

The revolutions of 1848 demonstrated to both liberals and conservatives that serious economic, social, and political problems must be examined and resolved. It was clearer to most that there were no simple solutions to the problems of industrial development. Many now agreed that insurrection and violence were not viable means of change. As the era passed, the revolutions of 1848 became an important reference point within the Western heritage.

IDENTIFICATIONS

Identify each one of the following as used in the text. Refer to the text as necessary.

	Text Page
proletarianization	515
confection	516
Chartism	516
"bobbies"	522
John Howard, Elizabeth Fry and Charles Lucas	522
Pentonville Prison	522
Iron Law of Wages	523
Anti-Corn Law League	524
Utopian Socialism	524
Auguste Blanqui	526
dictatorship of the proletariat	527
Alphonse Lamartine	528
General Cavaignac	529
"Little Napoleon"	529
Vesuvians	529
Voix des femmes	530
Louis Kossuth	530
First Pan Slavic Congress	531
Pius IX	532
Frankfurt Parliament	533-534
grossdeutsch vs. *kleindeutsch*	534

MAP EXERCISE A

Outline the boundaries of the European states at the mid-nineteenth century point. Mark the urban centers of revolution for the 1848-1849 period.

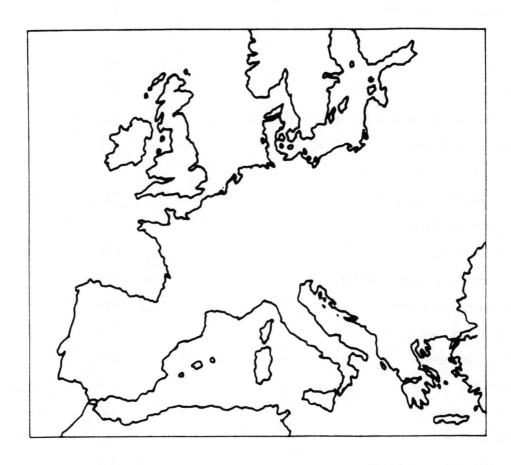

MAP EXERCISE B

Draw a map outlining the contemporary boundaries of France. Include the major geographical features, rivers, mountain ranges, etc. Include water boundaries and mark the borders with other European states.

SHORT-ANSWER EXERCISES

Multiple-Choice

_____ 1. Which of the following did not contribute to the industrial strength of Great Britain in the nineteenth century: (a) natural resources, (b) German technological advances, (c) adequate financial resources, (d) considerable mobility within society.

_____ 2. The largest railroad network in Europe before 1850 could be found in: (a) England, (b) France, (c) Belgium, (d) Germany.

_____ 3. Which of the following groups would not be considered a part of the early nineteenth-century labor force: (a) urban artisans and factory workers, (b) shopkeepers and inventors, (c) farm workers and countryside peddlers, (d) the working poor.

_____ 4. Which of the following would not be considered part of the Chartist reform program: (a) women's rights, (b) annual election of the House of Commons, (c) universal manhood suffrage, (d) salaries for Members of Parliament.

_____ 5. Which of the following is the most correct statement about the process of industrialization as it effected women: (a) women could now become the head of households, (b) women would have less control over family finances, (c) there were less opportunities created for many young women in work and marriage, (d) none of these is correct.

_____ 6. Apparently, the real reason for the repeal of the British Corn Laws was: (a) both rich and poor wanted corn from American farms, (b) the famine in Ireland, (c) it would appease the radical wing of the Chartist movement, (d) it would immediately reduce wages of factory workers.

_____ 7. Which of the following was not a major source of Karl Marx's ideas? (a) German Hegelianism, (b) utopian socialism, (c) French socialism, (d) British economic theory.

_____ 8. Demands of French women's groups during the revolution of 1848 included all of the following except: (a) religious freedom, (b) economic security, (c) educational opportunities, (d) the right to vote.

_____ 9. (a) Alphonse Lamartine, (b) Friedrich Engels, (c) Louis Blanc, (d) Louis Kossuth, led the Hungarian uprising against the Hapsburgs in 1848-1850.

_____ 10. Which of the following is not associated with the conservative reaction to the revolutions of 1848? (a) General Garibaldi, (b) General Cavaignac, (c) General Radetzky, (d) General Windischgrätz.

True-False

_____ 1. By the middle of the nineteenth century England was the most populous country of Europe.

_____ 2. The most dramatic application of steam technology was in the growth of railroads in Europe.

_____ 3. Among the Chartist reforms were demands for salaries for elected members of the House of Commons.

_____ 4. Though there were many eighteenth-century textile related inventions, it was the mechanization of weaving that had the greatest effect on the methods of work.

_____ 5. The least likely early employment occupation for a young woman was domestic service.

_____ 6. One of the theories of a policed society is that the visibility of law enforcement personnel will in itself deter crime.

_____ 7. Unlike the system developed at New York's Auburn prison, the Philadelphia system called for the complete isolation of the prisoners from each other.

_____ 8. The major European utopian socialists expected their reforming ideas to prevail as a result of mass revolutions by the workers.

_____ 9. While no single condition could have caused the upheavals of 1848 widespread food shortages and unemployment are factors to be considered.

_____ 10. Feminist efforts in France during the mid-century revolutions there led to near full acceptance of their agenda.

Completion

1. By the middle of the nineteenth century half the population of _____ lived in an urban setting.

2. One of the founders of the Chartist Movement was _____.

3. The now famous _Essay on the Principal of Population_ first appearing in 1798 was written by _____.

4. The earliest of the utopian socialists was _____.

5. The socialist experiment at New Harmony, Indiana (U.S.A.) was established by _____.

6. Charles Fourier's discussion of _____ was an early indication of a problem still confronting modern economic life.

7. Though the son of a middle-class factory owner, _____ was a close friend and fellow revolutionary of Karl Marx.

8. For _____ the victory of the proletariat over the bourgeoisie represented the culmination of human history.

9. King Charles Albert of _____ led an early effort to rid northern Italy of Austrian domination.

10. The Frankfurt Parliament made little headway on the issue of German _____.

FOR FURTHER CONSIDERATION

1. Within a general discussion of the rise of industrialization in Europe, what do the authors mean by the statement, "Industrialism grew on itself" (p. 514)?

2. Discuss the changing nature of the family in the first half of the nineteenth century. Note the role of industrialization in the lives of men, women, and children. Support your ideas fully.

3. Compare and contrast the utopian socialist ideas of Saint-Simon, Owen, and Fourier.

4. Define Marxism. Realistically what were Marx's goals within the framework of his idea of the proletarian revolution?

5. Briefly review the revolutionary events of 1848 in France, Italy, Austria, and Germany. How is it that Russia and Great Britain were untouched by the contagion of revolution in this period? After achieving some initial successes, most of the revolutionary movements of 1848 failed. Why?

ANSWERS

Multiple-Choice

		Text Page
1.	B	512
2.	A	514
3.	B	514-515
4.	A	516
5.	D	520-521
6.	B	524
7.	B	527
8.	A	530
9.	D	530
10.	A	529-532

True-False

1.	F	513
2.	T	514
3.	T	516
4.	T	517
5.	F	519
6.	T	522
7.	T	522
8.	F	525-526
9.	T	528
10.	F	530

Completion

1.	England/Wales	513
2.	William Lovett	516
3.	Thomas Malthus	523
4.	Count Saint-Simon	524
5.	Robert Owen	525
6.	boredom	525
7.	Friedrich Engels	526
8.	Karl Marx	527
9.	Piedmont	531
10.	unification	534

◆ ◆ ◆ ◆ ◆ ◆ ◆

THE AGE OF NATION-STATES

COMMENTARY

In the third quarter of the nineteenth century, the major states of Europe resolved basic problems that had been in evidence well before the revolutions of 1848. Despite the failure of those revolutionary movements, many of the ideas associated with them, and thereby with liberalism and nationalism, became reality in less than two decades.

An important stimulant to these many changes was the Crimean War. This seemingly unimportant conflict initiated by Russia and Ottoman Turkey in the mid-1850s had several side effects that pointed to a major reshuffling of what had been the powers of the Concert of Europe. At the same time the Crimean War suggested that internal social and economic reforms were in order and were indeed necessary to preserve the future of several states. In this same sense the unification of Italy (1861) and Germany (1871) represent major events in modern history. Much of the political history of Europe through 1945, if not 1990, can be directly traced not only to these unification movements but to many other facets of this same era. The success of Piedmont and Prussia in carrying out the unification movements was sustained by influential leaders (Cavour and Bismarck) and by related economic, social, and political reforms at home. The culmination of German unity in the Franco-Prussian War can be viewed as foreshadowing World War I nearly fifty years later.

France's difficulties during this same period kept that nation off balance as a series of political experiments, which had started in 1848, each ran its course. The reign of Emperor Napoleon III (Louis Napoleon Bonaparte), followed by the formation of the Third Republic, serves to illustrate the turmoil in French political life. The Dreyfus Affair furnished the most notable example of how unsettled France's sociopolitical life really was.

For the Austrian Empire this was an age of uncertain compromises. To deal with the ever-present national minorities, the Hapsburg government resorted to almost any plan that would sustain the Austro-German domination of the state. Admitting the Hungarian Magyars to a position of responsibility after 1867 illustrates the problem, but did not provide the solution. Francis Joseph's exceptionally long reign only further underscored the encrusted nature of Austro-Hungarian political thought. Similarly Russian tsars in the latter half of the nineteenth century attempted to bring about minimal reform; but the efforts were short-lived and not necessarily to the advantage of the vast majority of Russian peasants. The long-awaited freeing of the serfs in reality had the effect of binding many more rigidly to landlord control than before they were "free." The result was the formation of several extremist groups such as the People's Will which resorted to often fanatical violence in the hopes of stimulating tsarist reform.

By the end of the century it was again England that was leading the way toward social and political reform. Britain's early lead in industrialization nurtured an equally early lead, and under less pressure, in achieving a successful operation of liberal democracy at home while at the same time pursuing a wide-ranging foreign policy. The Great Reform Bill of 1867 became the beacon for the many reforms that followed. Capable leadership combined with an aloofness from continental problems gave Britain a clear advantage and success in many areas of European life. The Irish Question remained the exception because of its complexity and because of the historic bitterness that Home Rule and the Catholic Question represented.

By the 1870s the European state system had been transformed from what had been states characterized by an eighteenth-century outlook to nations, those recently established as well as the old, altered by visions of liberalism and nationalism. The stage was now set for heightened competition between the European states and as never before for the Europeans to dominate much of the world.

IDENTIFICATIONS

Identify each one of the following as used in the text. Refer to the text as necessary.

	Text Page
romantic republicanism	539
meeting at Plombières	540
Italia Irredenta	542
Count Vincent Benedetti	545
Battle of Sedan	546
Paris Commune	547
Marshal MacMahon	547
George Boulanger	547
"neoabsolutism"	549
October Diploma	549-550
Alexander Herzen	555
Vera Zasulich	555
People's Will	556
Reform Act of 1867	556
Public Health Act/Artisans Dwelling Act of 1875	557
Irish Land League	558
Home Rule Bill	558

MAP EXERCISE A

On this map of Italy, locate each of the following areas and cities.

Kingdom of the Two Sicilies
Piedmont
Lombardy
Papal States
Corsica

Sardinia
Brescia
Turin
Milan
Palermo
Naples

MAP EXERCISE B

On this map of Germany, locate each of the following areas and cities.

Jutland Peninsula	Schleswig-Holstein
France	Alsace-Lorraine
Denmark	Belgium
Prussia	Munich
Bavaria	Berlin

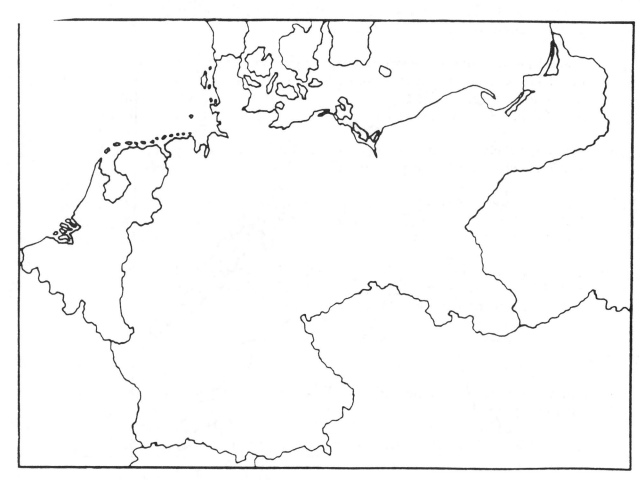

SHORT-ANSWER EXERCISES

Multiple-Choice

_____ 1. Which is the most accurate statement concerning the Crimean War: (a) both sides had well-equipped armies, (b) after the war instability prevailed in Europe for several decades, (c) the Concert of Europe ended, (d) there was no formal peace treaty to end the war.

_____ 2. The person most responsible for the final unification of Italy in 1861 was: (a) Niccolò Machiavelli, (b) Guiseppe Garibaldi, (c) Camillo Cavour, (d) Felice Orsini.

_____ 3. During the 1860s the Papal States were guarded by the troops of: (a) Piedmont, (b) Austria, (c) France, (d) Prussia.

_____ 4. The correct chronological order of Bismarck's moves leading to the unification of Germany was in victories against: (a) Denmark, Austria, France, (b) Austria, Denmark, France, (c) France, Denmark, Austria, (d) France, Austria, Denmark.

_____ 5. The immediate origins of the Franco-Prussian War lie in troubles within the monarchy of: (a) Prussia, (b) France, (c) Spain, (d) Denmark.

_____ 6. Which of the following occurred the earliest: (a) the secret conference at Plombières, (b) the death of Cavour, (c) formation of the North German Confederation, (d) Treaty of Frankfurt.

_____ 7. A politician who acquired considerable prestige in France's turbulent politics of the 1880s and who might have led a successful coup against the Third Republic was: (a) Adolphe Thiers, (b) George Boulanger, (c) Marshal MacMahon, (d) Leon Gambetta.

_____ 8. Before the 1860s the usual period of service for Russian military recruits was: (a) 6 months, (b) 5 years, (c) 10 years, (d) 25 years.

_____ 9. The Russian monarch Alexander III: (a) freed the serfs, (b) was a thoroughgoing reformer, (c) was the grandfather of Nicholas II, (d) was autocratic and reactionary.

_____ 10. Two of the most important Prime Ministers of England during the 1860s and 1870s were: (a) Peel and Derby, (b) Disraeli and Gladstone, (c) Palmerston and Aberdeen, (d) Cross and Russell.

True-False

_____ 1. The best known romantic republican of this era was Victor Emmanuel III of Piedmont-Sardinia.

_____ 2. The June 24, 1859 Battle at Solferino concluded the process of Italian unification.

_____ 3. When his brother Frederick William IV was judged insane, William I effectively became the ruler of Prussia.

_____ 4. Otto von Bismarck believed that German unification could be accomplished through Prussia's conservative constitution.

_____ 5. At the end of the Franco-Prussian War Louis Napoleon III was put on display in the Hall of Mirrors at Versailles Palace.

_____ 6. One of the announced goals of the Paris Commune was "free love."

_____ 7. In 1871 the Bourbon claimant to the throne refused to accept the revolutionary flag of France and was therefore bypassed in favor of the formation of the Third French Republic.

_____ 8. Installed during the revolutions of 1848, the Habsburg Emperor of Austria ruled for the next 58 years.

_____ 9. In the last quarter of the last century territorial integrity became the single most important factor in defining a nation.

_____ 10. The Education Act of 1870 and the Ballot Act of 1872 should each be considered the outcome of British conservative politics.

Completion

1. _____ was the one nation outside of Piedmont that was particularly supportive of the movement for Italian unification.

2. A function of mid-century Italian politics, the policy of _____ was rooted in bribery and corruption.

3. In the 1860s _____ led a French-supported expedition against Mexico.

4. One of the most dramatic affairs of French life in the 1890s revolved around an army officer named _____.

5. *J'accuse* was written by _____.

6. _____ was the name given to the document that created the so-called Dual Monarchy.

7. The Russian nobility had a large role in affairs of local governance through the system of provincial councils known as _____.

8. A revolutionary movement supported by many students, intellectuals, and radicals in Russia was known as _____.

9. In part as a result of their leadership in obtaining the Second Reform Bill of 1867, the British _____ Party has dominated politics there to this day.

10. The leader of the movement for Irish Home Rule was _____.

FOR FURTHER CONSIDERATION

1. Examine the respective roles of the participants and neutrals in the Crimean War. Which countries gained/lost by their actions in the conflict? Explain your answer fully.

2. Compare and contrast the processes involved in the unification of Italy with those involved in the unification of Germany.

3. Discuss what you consider to be the basic weakness of the Austrian (later Austro-Hungarian) Empire during Francis Joseph's reign?

4. Throughout much of the nineteenth century why was England able to remain the most liberally progressive of the major European states?

5. Throughout much of the nineteenth century why did Russia remain among the most reactionary of the European states? Do any of the problems examined here relate to the contemporary situation in Russia?

ANSWERS

Multiple-Choice

		Text Page
1.	C	538
2.	C	539
3.	C	542
4.	A	544-545
5.	C	545
6.	A	*passim*
7.	B	547
8.	D	555
9.	D	556
10.	B	556-557

True-False

1.	F	539
2.	F	540
3.	T	543
4.	T	544
5.	F	546
6.	F	547
7.	T	547
8.	F	549
9.	F	551
10.	F	556-557

Completion

1.	France	540
2.	*transformismo*	542
3.	Archduke Maximilian of Austria	546
4.	Alfred Dreyfus	548
5.	Emile Zola	548
6.	*Ausgleich*/Compromise of 1867	550
7.	*zemstvos*	554
8.	Populism	555
9.	Conservative (Tory)	556
10.	Charles Stewart Parnell	558

THE BUILDING OF EUROPEAN SUPREMACY: SOCIETY AND POLITICS TO WORLD WAR I

COMMENTARY

The half century before the outbreak of World War I (1914-1918) clearly established the foundations upon which much of Western civilization now rests. The related growth of population, capitalism, industry, and urban centers was rapidly changing the European landscape and outlook by the last half of the nineteenth century. A significantly advanced phase of industrial development was for a second time revolutionizing the European world. Electricity, higher grade steel, and petrochemicals spurred new industries based upon resources and technologies that were more than mere forerunners of today's industrial maturity. Large corporations, cartels, and multinational business interests were transferring the older economic principles into our own modem concepts. These facts alone caused a widespread reappraisal of social, economic, and political life.

Governments and their industrial powers were more ready than ever to serve each other's mutual needs. A new social consciousness emerged and was coupled directly to the growth of an ambitious and energetic middle class. The roles of women and children within this rising class set a pattern not changed until our own time, and still not entirely changed. For example, recent research better explains the expectations and roles of working and middle-class women. Equally interesting is how current studies of prostitution in this era counter some of the myths associated with this occupation. Although the position of the working classes was still inferior, many workers now enjoyed a way of life and a standard of living that easily eclipsed that of the previous half century. Notable among these benefits were the efforts in city planning and reconstruction that were designed to advance the nation's commercial interests and enhance the living environs of the various social classes. There were additional indications that the economic growth and related benefits would continue for all classes of people.

Naturally these events were not without their tensions. Socialism moved from the pens of the theorists of the pre-1848 era to a position of acceptability and respectability throughout much of Europe. At the same time the many versions of socialism were constantly debated throughout the times, and their many and wide-ranging interpretations prevented the socialists from achieving a united front. This pattern, however, differed in each nation of Europe. In Britain, where political compromise and accommodation were an already accepted and popular mode of resolving conflict, Parliament sought change that at least moderately incorporated the ideas of the reformers.

On the continent less compromise can be seen. "Opportunism" in France received little acceptance. The French picture was further clouded by the bitterness of the struggle with the Paris Commune in 1871 and again throughout the Dreyfus Affair at the end of the century. In Germany, Bismarckian political maneuvers managed to keep the Social Democrats off guard until after 1900. Their socialist reform programs were often eclipsed by the overall growth and economic successes of that nation.

By the end of the century Russian socialism had emerged as the most radical continental movement. With Russia's late entrance into industrialization and agricultural reform, a situation exacerbated by the success evidenced in other nations, that country's progress was almost stillborn. Conservative-minded czars managed to stay in power by cultivating the nobility, controlling the relatively small commercial classes, and by sometimes ruthlessly quelling worker unrest—as in the Revolution of 1905.

On the eve of World War I, which came on the heels of dramatic economic growth in Europe socialist reform programs can be viewed as a mixture of successes and failures. But their programs and efforts, though temporarily stemmed by the war, were to be a permanent part of the Western heritage.

IDENTIFICATIONS

Identify each one of the following as used in the text. Refer to the text as necessary.

	Text Page
Henry Bessemer	561
Gottlieb Daimler	562
Henry Ford	562-563
Georges Haussmann	565
Married Woman's Property Act	569
Mary Wollstonecraft	573
Millicent Fawcett	574
Emmeline Pankhurst	574
Hubertine Auclert	574
BDFK	575
emancipation of Jews	575-576
Kier Hardie	578
Parliament Act of 1911	578
Opportunism	579
syndicalism	579
SPD	579
Erfurt Program of 1891	580
Eduard Bernstein	580
Gregory Plekhanov	581
P. A. Stolypin	582-583
Grigory Efimovich Rasputin	583

MAP EXERCISE A

On the accompanying map locate each of the capital cities of Europe:

105

CHAPTER 24
THE BUILDING OF
EUROPEAN SUPREMACY:
SOCIETY AND POLITICS TO
WORLD WAR I

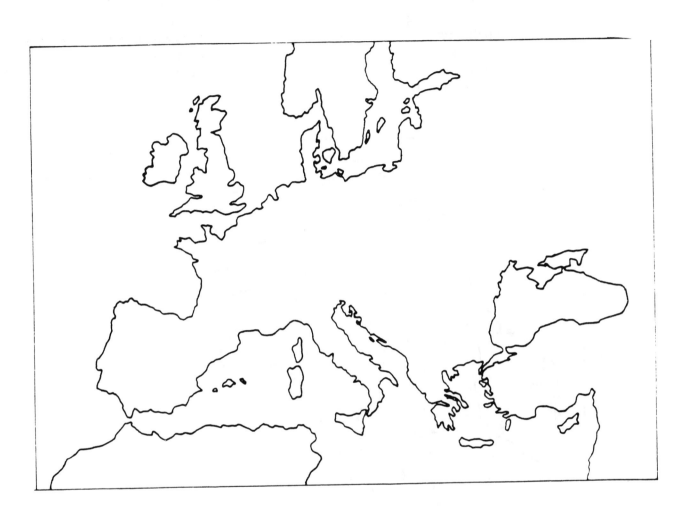

MAP EXERCISE B

On the accompanying map of Western Russia, show each of the following.

Gulf of Finland
Lake Ladoga
St. Petersburg
Baltic Sea
Finland
Black Sea
Crimean Peninsula

Ural Mountains
Moscow
Germany
Austria-Hungary
Sea of Azov
Dnieper River
Volga River

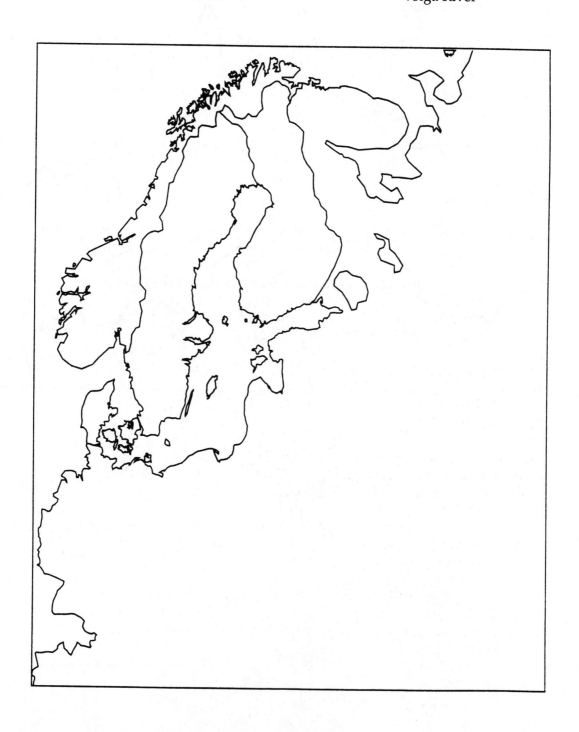

SHORT-ANSWER EXERCISES

107
CHAPTER 24
THE BUILDING OF
EUROPEAN SUPREMACY:
SOCIETY AND POLITICS TO
WORLD WAR I

Multiple-Choice

_____ 1.   Between 1860 and 1914: (a) Europe's financial and industrial supremacy emerged, (b) socialism became an influential part of European political life, (c) the modern basis of the welfare state emerged in Europe, (d) all of these occurred.

_____ 2.   By 1910 the population of Europe reached nearly: (a) 600 million, (b) 450 million, (c) 300 million, (d) 150 million.

_____ 3.   Which of the following is the most accurate statement about the development of European cities in the second half of the nineteenth century: (a) the central portions of many major cities were redesigned, (b) residents began to look for housing outside of city centers, (c) commercialization of city centers took place, (d) all of these.

_____ 4.   Important new medical practices became a part of European life in this era because of the research of all of the following, except: (a) Georges Haussmann in France, (b) Robert Koch in Germany, (c) Joseph Lister in Britain, (d) Louis Pasteur in France.

_____ 5.   The most advanced women's movement in Europe could be found in: (a) Austro-Hungarian Empire, (b) Great Britain, (c) France, (d) the Netherlands.

_____ 6.   Which of the following is the most correct statement about trades unions by 1900: (a) they were completely suppressed in Germany, (b) most members were unskilled laborers, (c) they were legalized in Germany, England, and France, (d) only Great Britain permitted their existence.

_____ 7.   The collapse of the First International is least attributed to: (a) the success of British unionism, (b) the growth and influence of other socialist organizations, (c) events surrounding the Paris Commune, (d) moving its headquarters to the United States.

_____ 8.   The type of socialism that aimed at gradual and peaceful change within the existing social-political framework was known as: (a) trade unionism, (b) Marxism, (c) Fabianism, (d) syndicalism.

_____ 9.   Bismarck's response to the efforts of the German socialists was: (a) a repression of the socialist parties, (b) health insurance, (c) government-sponsored social welfare programs, (d) all of these.

_____ 10.   The most notable Russian Marxists of the nineteenth century were: (a) Vladimir Ulyanov and Gregory Plekhanov, (b) Gregory Plekhanov and Eduard Bernstein, (c) Eduard Bernstein and Karl Kautsky, (d) Vladimir Lenin and Gregori Rasputin.

True-False

_____ 1. The out-migration of Europeans to the United States, Canada, South Africa, and Argentina had the effect of relieving social pressures on the Continent.

_____ 2. Concern for urban riots was among the factors which prompted Louis Napoleon's rebuilding of the city of Paris.

_____ 3. In the last half of the nineteenth century it became clear that new urban water and sewer systems would achieve considerable health benefits for the entire population.

_____ 4. From what we know, female prostitutes appear to have moved into the work force by the age of twenty-five.

_____ 5. Continuous demonstrations by the "suffragettes" brought British women the franchise in 1918.

_____ 6. Pogroms protected Jews from violence in Russia.

_____ 7. The First International did not last long and had little influence on European socialism.

_____ 8. For participating in a plot against Czar Alexander III, Lenin's older brother was executed in 1887.

_____ 9. "Bloody Sunday" was a 1905 event in which several thousand Russian workers and poor successfully attacked the Tzar's Winter Palace in Saint Petersburg.

_____ 10. The authors of the text assert that during the latter part of the nineteenth century Europe experienced the emergence of socialism, labor unions, contradictory life-styles, and growing demands of women in politics.

Completion

1. The growth of the chemical industry at the end of the nineteenth century was especially fostered by this nation _____.

2. The single most important aspect of the later industrial revolution was in the use of _____ for production.

3. After 1850 the _____ became the arbiter of consumer taste and defender of the status quo.

4. Model Industrial Communities were created by the German armament corporation _____.

5. _____ was a phrase used to depict instances of cooperation between French socialists and the government.

6. _____ was the author of *Evolutionary Socialism* (1899).

7. The person who led Russia into the industrial age was _____.

8. In Russia the more prosperous peasant farmers were known as _____.

9. Lenin's group within the Russian Social Democratic Party was known as the _____.

10. Instrumental in causing serious unrest in Russia in 1905 was that country's defeat by _____.

109
CHAPTER 24
THE BUILDING OF
EUROPEAN SUPREMACY:
SOCIETY AND POLITICS TO
WORLD WAR I

FOR FURTHER CONSIDERATION

1. Explain in detail the differences between the First and Second Industrial Revolutions.

2. Describe the position of women within the middle-class household and within society generally at the end of the nineteenth century.

3. Describe in detail the key elements of the feminist movement at the end of the nineteenth and into the early part of the twentieth century. Be sure to discuss the leading personalities of the movement and list their most important goals.

4. Compare and contrast any three of the non-Russian socialist theories of this era.

5. As exemplified in his pamphlet *What Is to Be Done?* what were Lenin's ideas and how were they different from the ideas of others in the Russian Social Democratic party?

ANSWERS

111

CHAPTER 24
THE BUILDING OF
EUROPEAN SUPREMACY:
SOCIETY AND POLITICS TO
WORLD WAR I

Multiple-Choice

		Text Page
1.	D	560-561
2.	B	561
3.	D	565
4.	A	568
5.	B	574
6.	C	576
7.	D	577
8.	C	578
9.	D	580
10.	A	581

True-False

1.	T	561
2.	T	565
3.	T	566-568
4.	T	571
5.	F	574
6.	F	575
7.	F	577
8.	T	581
9.	F	582
10.	T	583-584

Completion

1.	Germany	562
2.	electricity	562
3.	middle class	564
4.	Krupp	568
5.	Opportunism	579
6.	Eduard Bernstein	580
7.	Sergei Witte	581
8.	*kulaks*	581
9.	Bolsheviks	582
10.	Japan	582

◆ ◆ ◆ ◆ ◆ ◆ ◆

Chapter 25

THE BIRTH OF CONTEMPORARY EUROPEAN THOUGHT

COMMENTARY

Any adequate understanding of the world we live in today requires serious consideration and thorough understanding of those strains of thought associated with the turn of the nineteenth century. The changes that occurred in scientific and intellectual thinking and outlook during Europe's Victorian era should not be underestimated.

These changes were stimulated by an increasingly literate and better-educated public. The increase in education, coupled with wider and cheaper means of printing and distribution, brought men and women all over Europe in touch with the scientific and intellectual community as never before. This contact, however, was also to introduce the general public mind to many iconoclastic viewpoints that further increased the social and political tensions of the era.

As in a previous period of Western history, it was science that initially stimulated new outlooks. The mechanistic principles of nature established during the Enlightenment underwent considerable transformation. Theories of evolution, related racial theories, modern atomic principles, and Freudian psychology, combined with an ever-increasing view of the ability of science to solve all humankind's problems, shattered many ideas long accepted. The organized churches of Europe were assaulted from several sides and placed on the defensive as never before. Christianity now found itself in opposition to much of what was happening. Many governments, inspired by religion's defensive posture, made inroads on a number of previously accepted areas of church authority. In Germany this assault was highlighted by Bismarck's *Kulturkampf*. The most powerful religious organization, the Roman Catholic Church, under Popes Pius IX and Leo XIII, had exceptional difficulties in adapting to the new scientific and intellectual positions. Yet by the end of the era most church organizations remained as viable parts of Europe's social, political, and cultural life.

This era is notable for the widespread social criticism that was stimulated by the scientific ferment and enunciated by articulate writers. A new "realism" in literature, which criticized almost all romantic notions, left no stone unturned in examining the less savory areas of human endeavor in the industrial age. Poverty, prostitution, and the bourgeois family with its hapless female adjuncts were all subjects for critical examination.

Not only were society, industrial life, and culture attacked, but with Nietzsche and other irrationalist writers the whole basis of the new criticism itself, reason, was challenged. For Nietzsche the philosophical assumptions of all Western civilization were wrong and in serious need of re-evaluation. The birth of contemporary European thought is clearly seen with the advent of Freud's teachings. As Marx had previously caused a re-examination of the capitalist system and Darwin fostered a reassessment of major biological assumptions, Freud forced a serious look at the role of the subconscious. These three seminal thinkers, interpreting the new dimensions of human life, ushered in the world as we know it.

It is also clear today that the Feminist movement which emerged after World War II had roots in the modernist literary atmosphere of the late Nineteenth century. Over-shadowed by the events of two world wars the contemporary movement, although still defining itself, is another sign of the rich intellectual heritage of the pre-World War I era.

During this era men and women challenged many of the underlying assumptions upon which western thought was founded. Their works, despite the frequent criticism and constant re-evaluation, remain basic to any competent understanding of the western heritage today.

IDENTIFICATIONS

Identify each one of the following as used in the text. Refer to the text as necessary.

	Text Page
Le Petit Journal and *Daily Mail*	587
Auguste Comte	588
Gregor Mendel	589
"ethical imperative" of Herbert Spencer	591
Catholic Modernism	595
Ernst Mach and Henri Poincaré	595
Wilhelm Roentgen	595
"uncertainty principle"	596
Madame Bovary	597
Henrik Ibsen	597
Igor Stravinsky	598
Bloomsbury Group	598
Thus Spoke Zarathrustra	599
id, ego, and superego	601
Max Weber	602
Georges Sorel	602
Aryans	602
Houston Stewart Chamberlain	602
Karl Lueger	603
Theodor Herzl	603
Karen Horney and Melanie Klein	604
Contagious Diseases Act	604
A Room of One's Own	605

MAP EXERCISE

On the map following this list place the boundaries and names of the European countries; within those boundaries place the number for the name of the person listed. You should use the country of birth; but in some cases the place of work should be noted. You may need to consult other sources.

1.	Joseph Breuer	19.	Friedrich Nietzsche
2.	Houston S. Chamberlain	20.	Vilfredo Pareto
3.	Auguste Comte	21.	Max Planck
4.	Charles Darwin	22.	Pope Leo XIII
5.	Albert Einstein	23.	Ernst Renan
6.	Auguste Ficke	24.	Wilhelm Roentgen
7.	Sigmund Freud	25.	Ernest Rutherford
8.	Arthur de Gobineau	26.	George Bernard Shaw
9.	Thomas Henry Huxley	27.	William Robertson Smith
10.	Ernst Haeckel	28.	Herbert Spencer
11.	Theodor Herzl	29.	Lytton Strachey
12.	Henrik Ibsen	30.	David Friedrich Strauss
13.	Carl Jung	31.	J. J. Thomson
14.	Julius Langbehn	32.	Karl Vogt
15.	Karl Lueger	33.	Alfred Russel Wallace
16.	Charles Lyell	34.	Max Weber
17.	Karl Marx	35.	Julius Wellhausen
18.	Gregor Mendel	36.	Virginia Woolf

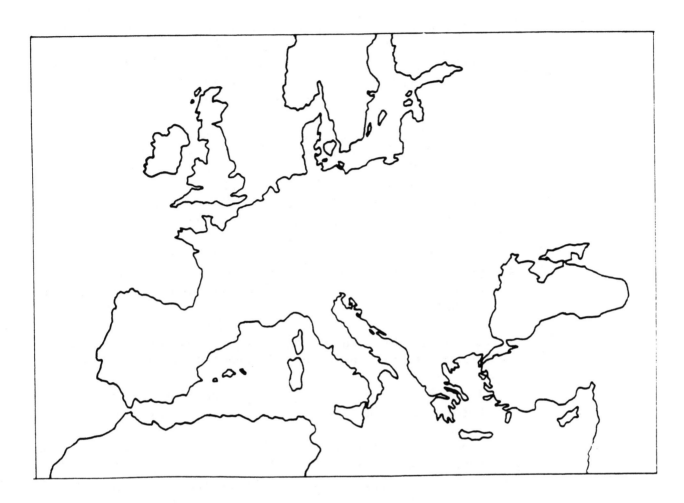

Multiple-Choice

_____ 1.   By the turn of the century which of the following European states had the highest literacy rate: (a) Spain, (b) Austria-Hungary, (c) Belgium, (d) Italy.

_____ 2.   Three stages of human development—theological, metaphysical, and positivist—stem from the thought of: (a) Émile Durkheim, (b) Auguste Comte, (c) Thomas Henry Huxley, (d) Claude Bernard.

_____ 3.   (a) Julius Wellhausen, (b) David Friederich Strauss, (c) William Robertson Smith, (d) Ernst Renan in his *Life of Jesus* cast doubt on the origins of Christianity.

_____ 4.   The dogma of the infallibility of the pope in matters of faith and morals stems from the: (a) concept of Catholic Modernism, (b) First Vatican Council, (c) *Rerum Novarum*, (d) *Syllabus of Errors*.

_____ 5.   Pope Leo XIII's encyclical *Rerum Novarum* supported all of the following except: (a) just wages, (b) private property, (c) socialism, (d) religious education.

_____ 6.   (a) Wilhelm Roentgen, (b) Henri Becquerel, (c) Max Planck, (d) Ernest Rutherford is considered to have discovered x-rays.

_____ 7.   The word "overman" is most clearly associated with the thinking of: (a) Friedrich Nietzsche, (b) Pope Pius XI, (c) George Gissing, (d) Émile Zola.

_____ 8.   "The dream is a fulfillment of a wish" would be a phrase best associated with: (a) Friedrich Nietzsche, (b) Max Planck, (c) Sigmund Freud, (d) Leo Tolstoy.

_____ 9.   Which of the following names would not be considered as that of an anti-Semitic writer or politician? (a) Theodor Herzl, (b) Adolf Stoecker, (c) Karl Lueger, (d) Houston S. Chamberlain.

_____ 10.   With *A Room of One's Own* Virginia Woolf opened: (a) a new discussion of sexual morality, (b) the whole question of gender definition, (c) an assault against the male dominated literary world, (d) demands for living space for single women.

True-False

_____ 1.   Intellectual life in the last half of the nineteenth century was altered by the existence of a mass reading audience.

_____ 2.   In 1830 Charles Lyell established the basis of the modern theory of chemical composition.

_____ 3. The replacement of the Falloux Law of 1850 with the so-called Ferry Laws effectively removed religious education from the public schools of France.

_____ 4. At the turn of the century both Max Planck and Albert Einstein were challenging the conventional theories of physics.

_____ 5. In his *Androcles and the Lion* George Bernard Shaw praised Christianity's role throughout the ages.

_____ 6. Friedrich Nietzsche whose first important philosophical work was titled *The Birth of Tragedy* was actually trained in the study of ancient literary texts.

_____ 7. The Austrian physician Sigmund Freud believed that the innocence of childhood, particularly in regard to sexual things, should be preserved with great care until at least puberty.

_____ 8. Carl Jung's work challenged Freud's views on dreams and the primacy of sexuality.

_____ 9. Arthur de Gobineau's theories of racial determinism expressed in his *Essay on the Inequality of the Human Races* noted that the process of degeneration would end within a century.

_____ 10. The idea that the Jews should establish their own nation (Zionism) is associated with the work of Theodor Herzl.

Completion

1. _____ was the scientist who first began to unravel the mystery of heredity.

2. The terms "evolutionary ethics" and "social Darwinism" are associated with the works of _____.

3. Pope Pius IX's issuance of the _____ was a clear sign of the Church's antiliberal stance.

4. Gustave Flaubert's _____ is often considered the first genuinely realistic novel.

5. In the play _____ George Bernard Shaw explored the matter of prostitution.

6. An example of painters adopting musical titles for their work would be J.A.M. Whistler's _____ .

7. The need to create a new moral order based on pride, assertiveness, and strength is associated with the writings of _____ .

8. _____ was a student of Freud who later could not accept the idea that sex played the prime role in the formation of the human personality.

9. *The Protestant Ethic and the Spirit of Capitalism* was written by _____ .

10. There was a notable revival of _____ during the last third of the nineteenth century.

FOR FURTHER CONSIDERATION

1. Discuss several factors that gave rise to increased literacy in Europe by the end of the nineteenth century. Why was the increase in literacy so important to the intellectual and scientific developments of the era?

2. Examine the broad-based attacks upon the Christian churches in the late nineteenth century. What were the origins of these challenges to religious authority? What were the results?

3. Describe the views of the German writer Friedrich Nietzsche. Are his views relevant or irrelevant today?

4. How do you assess the impact of the works of Sigmund Freud? What were the chief positions taken in his pioneering studies?

5. Discuss the foundations of the Feminist movement at the turn of the century? Why was there an insistence upon defining gender roles?

ANSWERS

Multiple-Choice

		Text Page
1.	C	587
2.	B	588
3.	B	591
4.	B	594
5.	C	594
6.	A	595-596
7.	A	599
8.	C	600-601
9.	A	602-603
10.	B	605

True-False

1.	T	587
2.	F	592
3.	T	593
4.	T	596
5.	F	597
6.	T	599
7.	F	600
8.	T	601
9.	F	602
10.	T	603

Completion

1.	Gregor Mendel	589
2.	Herbert Spencer	591
3.	*Syllabus of Errors*	594
4.	*Madame Bovary*	597
5.	*Mrs. Warren's Profession*	597
6.	*Nocturnes*	598
7.	Friedrich Nietzsche	600
8.	Carl Jung	601
9.	Max Weber	602
10.	anti-Semitism	603

◆ ◆ ◆ ◆ ◆ ◆ ◆

For Further Consideration of the Documents

Each of the following questions is designed to help you reach a better understanding of certain of the original documents presented in the last five chapters of the text. Feel free to use the page numbers provided to refer back to the document as necessary. The value of a primary historical source should not be underestimated; it helps us understand the nature of the era in which it was written.

Mazzini on Nationalism (pp. 490-491)

1. Do you agree with this definition? How can nationalism be defined in a multi-cultural, multi-ethnic (multi-racial), or multi-linguistic context? Explain your answer fully.

Women Explain Their Situation (pp. 520-521)

2. Re-cast the complaints written here in terms of the circumstances that women face in today's work place?

Lord Acton Condemns Nationalism (p. 552)

3. "The theory of nationality, therefore, is a retrograde step in history." Having reviewed Lord Acton's analysis, do you agree or disagree with him? Explain your answer fully and use contemporary examples as necessary.

A Working Class Slum (p. 567)

4. Where would you find such a disturbing scene today? Should government be responsible for the improvement of such conditions? Fully explain your answer.

Darwin's View of Nature (p. 590)

5. How does Darwin ennoble the human species? Do you agree or disagree with his position?

Chapter 26

IMPERIALISM, ALLIANCES, AND WAR

COMMENTARY

The economic and technological advances made within the European system virtually Europeanized the world by the end of the nineteenth century. Never before had one section of the globe held such far-reaching authority over another. And the situation was evident to peoples at both ends of this "new Imperialism." The process of modern European development, normally associated with the Renaissance, the Scientific Revolution, and the Enlightenment, had resulted in the demonstrable European superiority. From their superior position the great powers of Europe, and somewhat belatedly Japan, were able to reach out and establish colonial control over less-developed, nonindustrial areas. This colonializing process was most evident on the African continent; there competition between the European states was a factor that drove on the explorers, missionaries, traders, bankers, and politicians. The conditions of this "new Imperialism," unlike those of earlier periods of international competition, engaged all sectors of a nation's social, economic, and political life. This engagement intensified the already stimulated sense of nationalism felt in Europe. As a result, by 1900 the European states were practically realigned into a bipolar alliance system. And, in retrospect, there were clear signs—Italy and France in North Africa; Austria and Russia in the Balkans; France and England in Central Africa; Germany and England in East Africa; Japan, China, and Russia in Asia—that imperialist concerns could lead to steadily increasing serious confrontations.

Recognizing these factors, the great powers looked to their armies and navies as more necessary than ever before. Consequently militarism, as a condition of life, became a norm. The acceleration of technological development greatly increased military needs, expenditures, and training programs as the developing alliance system demanded larger armed forces. Imperial concerns, coupled with increased rivalries between the great powers, called forth the new alliance system in Europe inaugurated by the Austro-German (Dual) Alliance of 1879.

The smashing success of Germany in defeating France and establishing the German Empire changed the nature of European power politics. The unification of Germany, unlike that of Italy, was a success virtually from the start. The weaknesses often associated with newly formed states were not apparent in the new German Empire. The defeat of France and the establishment of the German Empire set in motion a chain of events not entirely concluded even today. The destiny of France was immediately tied to avenging this "humiliation" by Germany. For the satisfied German government, under the masterful influence of Bismarck, the future lay in maintaining the status quo, developing to Germany's benefit the enormous gains that were a part of the French defeat and the German unification. In less than a decade, however, the European states were moved into an ever-widening consideration of rivalries as a result of their extension into Africa and Asia. For the Austro-Hungarian Empire and the Russian Empire this expansive mood brought conflicts closer to home in the crumbling European empire of the Ottoman Turks—the Balkans. Here an infectious nationalism centered in Serbia and Bulgaria caused growing unrest. The Russian intervention there that led to the 1878 Congress of Berlin was a forerunner of future problems. By the 1890s Germany, Austria-Hungary, and Italy had formed the Triple Alliance, and France and Russia had been drawn together in a mutual defense pact. In 1902 Britain left behind her "splendid isolation" to form an alliance with Japan. Then she was drawn into the Franco-Russian orbit, forming the *Entente Cordiale* with France in 1904 and a similar agreement with Russia in 1907.

Though imperial rivalries continued world-wide, the unresolved problem through the early 1900s was the Balkans. Conflicts between the Balkan nationalities themselves, the weakness of the Ottoman Empire, and the conflicting ambitions of Russia and Austria left the area with an unclosable wound. In this context the assassination of the Austrian heir in June 1914 at Sarajevo proved catastrophic. The chain of events that followed, the competition, the fears, the misunderstandings of the previous half century, quickly transformed the Balkan crisis into the immediate cause of World War I.

For 51 months the military of the European states slugged it out on battlefields and seas throughout the world. Before the war ended over 30 states were involved, including the United States, and the casualties totaled over 30 million. The European world, so safe, secure, and stable, had blown up. The task of repairing the damage of so great a conflict fell on the shoulders of mere mortals, who as heads of state had to follow their political instincts, their people's demands, and not always their consciences. The Peace of Paris, the Versailles settlement, was the product of long labor but was negotiated under such embittered conditions that the peacemakers' treaty became a problem even before it was completed. Too much had changed in such a short period of time, and errors were made that were destined to haunt future generations.

The decision not to include Germany in the Peace Conference was a fateful one because it left the door wide open to future uncertainty It was similarly unwise to exclude the Soviet Union. To ignore so great a revolution as had occurred in Russia was at least short sighted. The great Russian state had entered the war with mixed emotions, uncertain in direction, with a weakened military machine, serious political and economic problems, and a populace no longer convinced of the czar's authority. For that country to have sent its soldiers against the best army in Europe was itself a travesty. By 1917 revolutions in Russia had brought the Bolsheviks under Lenin to power. What would have seemed inconceivable three years before was a reality. Russia was to be transformed. Lenin's slogan of "Bread, Peace, and Land" won him sufficient support that when coupled with an unchecked ruthlessness, a sign of things to come in this century, the Bolsheviks had complete control of the state by 1921.

In the early 1920's the Bolsheviks busied themselves in securing what they envisioned to be the Soviet future. A process today seemingly in reverse. The world once so clearly dominated by western Europe would soon experience the strains awakened by radical ideologies emerging at wars end. The Europeans themselves, so confident a generation before, faced new uncertainties that undermined what security remained in the aftermath of World War I.

IDENTIFICATIONS

Identify each one of the following as used in the text refer to the text as necessary.

	Text Page
"New Imperialism"	609
Treaty of San Stefano	615
A "place in the sun"	617
the Boers	618
Entente Cordiale	618
Sir Edward Grey	619
"Young Turks"	620
the "Panther"	620
"dreadnought"	620
Balkan Crisis of 1913	621
Conrad von Hötzendorf	622
"the lights were going out all over Europe"	623
Schlieffen Plan	624
Erich Ludendorff	624
Erich von Falkenhayn	627
Lusitania	627
Duma	629
Leon Trotsky	630
Treaty of Brest-Litovsk	631
Fourteen Points	631-632
"Big Four"	632
Philipp Scheidmann	636

MAP EXERCISE A

Name/locate the major bodies of water surrounding the African continent.

Devise a color or shading scheme to show the areas of European colonial control throughout the African continent for each of the following states:

Great Britain
Germany
France
Belgium

Italy
Spain
Portugal

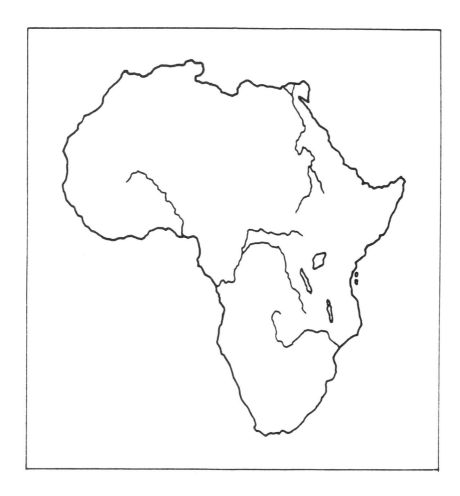

MAP EXERCISE B

Mark the appropriate boundaries of those eastern European countries which appeared at the end of World War I.

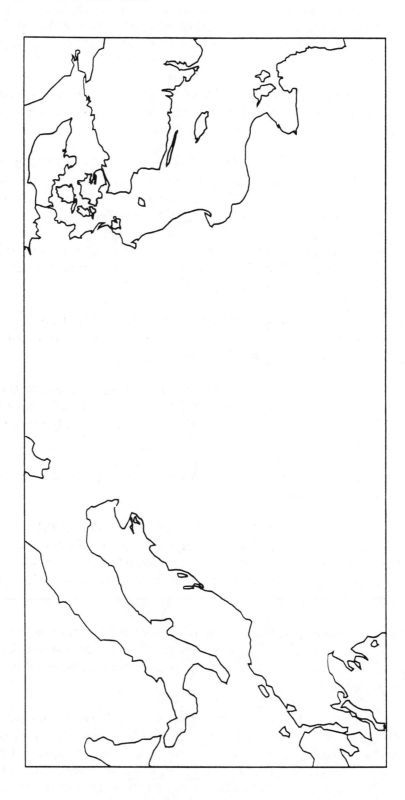

Multiple-Choice

_____ 1. German imperialism in this era was motivated by the need: (a) for profit, (b) to gain international prestige, (c) to obtain access to strategic waterways, (d) to divert attention from Germany's position on the continent.

_____ 2. Which of the following areas was the least vulnerable to European expansion at the end of the nineteenth-century? (a) China, (b) South America, (c) Ottoman Empire, (d) Africa.

_____ 3. Which of the following is not a result of the Congress of Berlin of 1878: (a) Austria-Hungary "gained" the provinces of Bosnia and Herzegovina, (b) Germany and Russia would soon drift further apart, (c) Bulgaria was reduced in size, (d) all of these were the results of the meeting.

_____ 4. The three states of the Triple Alliance were: (a) Germany, Russia, and Austria-Hungary, (b) Great Britain, France, and Russia, (c) Germany, Austria-Hungary, and Italy, (d) Russia, France, and Serbia.

_____ 5. The three states of the Triple Entente were: (a) Germany, Russia, and Austria-Hungary, (b) Great Britain, France, and Russia, (c) Germany, Austria-Hungary, and Italy, (d) Russia, France, and Serbia.

_____ 6. Of all of the major powers involved, which of the two appear to have been most responsible for the outbreak of the World War I: (a) Great Britain and France, (b) Germany and Great Britain, (c) Russia and Austria-Hungary, (d) Germany and Austria.

_____ 7. Throughout the war the most effective basic new weapon was the: (a) machine gun, (b) tank, (c) submarine, (d) airplane.

_____ 8. Lenin and the Bolsheviks signed the Treaty of Brest-Litovsk in 1918 because: (a) Russia was not able to carry on the war effort, (b) Lenin's government needed time to impose its will on the Russian people, (c) Lenin believed that communism would soon sweep through the warring states of Europe, (d) all of these.

_____ 9. One of the factors that appeared to hasten the peacemakers at Paris to conclude the Treaty of Versailles was: (a) the threat of a renewed war with Germany, (b) the near collapse of France, (c) President Wilson's political problems at home, (d) none of these.

_____ 10. With regard to eastern Europe the settlements of the Paris Peace Conference included all of the following except: (a) Bulgaria was enlarged from territory of Greece and Yugoslavia, (b) the complete disappearance of the Austro-Hungarian Empire, (c) Finland, Estonia, Latvia, and Lithuania became independent states, (d) the Magyars were left in control of the new Hungarian state.

True-False

_____ 1.   A novel aspect of the so-called New Imperialism was the efforts of the imperial power to integrate the native inhabitants into the managerial structure of the colony.

_____ 2.   During this period the English statesman Joseph Chamberlain advanced the idea of overseas empires serving as a source of profit that could be utilized to finance domestic reform and welfare programs in the home country.

_____ 3.   The effort to keep France isolated in Europe was a cornerstone of Bismarck's policy.

_____ 4.   The First Moroccan Crisis was temporarily resolved at an 1906 international meeting held at Portsmouth, New Hampshire (U.S.A.)

_____ 5.   An integral part of the Second Moroccan Crisis was the British assumption that Germany was moving to establish a naval base there.

_____ 6.   Today it is clear that the plot against Archduke Francis Ferdinand was supported by high ranking persons within the Serbian army.

_____ 7.   At the time of the outbreak of World War I the mobilization of the armed forces of any country was interpreted as a bluff and not to be taken seriously.

_____ 8.   Italy was lured into World War I against Germany and Austria-Hungary as a result of territorial promises made by the Western Allies.

_____ 9.   Russian Mensheviks believed, like Karl Marx, that a proletarian revolution could occur only after the bourgeois stage of development.

_____ 10.   At the end of World War I a right-wing group emerged under the name of "Spartacus" and challenged the newly established government of Germany.

Completion

1.   In one word, hegemony means _____ .

2.   Probably the statesman least interested in establishing colonies in Africa was _____.

3.   The so-called _____ brought the empires of Germany, Russia, and Austria-Hungary together in 1873.

4.   _____ was the country that gained the least from the 1878 Congress of Berlin.

5.   Bismarck's successor in office was _____.

6.   The architect of the new German navy was _____.

7. It can be said that Britain's isolation ended with her treaty with _____.

8. Though neither side gained a decisive advantage, heavy fighting in 1916 centered on the French stronghold at _____.

9. _____ and _____ were nations both excluded from the newly formed League of Nations.

10. In the last analysis the German-Russian Treaty of _____ was more harsh than the arrangements made at the Paris Peace Conference respective to the Treaty of Versailles.

FOR FURTHER CONSIDERATION

1. Discuss several of the causes of the so-called "New Imperialism." In your opinion which countries in their colonial efforts gained an advantage and which countries gained little or nothing for-their efforts?

2. Give an overall year-by-year review of the important military strategies and events of World War I.

3. Describe the economic and political realities in Russia during World War I. In your opinion should Lenin and the Bolsheviks have been surprised at their seemingly sudden success? Explain your answer fully.

4. In an analysis of the results of the Versailles settlement list what can be considered as specific successes and failures of the Paris Peace Conference of 1919? Briefly explain each one.

5. Compare and contrast the conditions of European politics and society that existed at the time of the Congress of Vienna (1815) with those existing at the time of the Paris Peace Conference (1919).

ANSWERS

Multiple-Choice

		Text Page
1.	B	611
2.	B	613
3.	D	615
4.	C	615-616
5.	B	617-619
6.	C	621-623
7.	A	624
8.	D	631
9.	D	633
10.	A	635

True False

1.	F	609
2.	T	611
3.	T	615
4.	F	619
5.	T	620
6.	T	621
7.	F	623
8.	T	626
9.	T	630
10.	F	633

Completion

1.	influence/authority	609
2.	Otto von Bismarck	611
3.	Three Emperors' League	615
4.	Germany	615
5.	Leo von Caprivi	617
6.	Alfred von Tirpitz	618
7.	Japan	618
8.	Verdun	627
9.	Russia/Soviet Union and Germany	633
10.	Brest-Litovsk	636 and 631

Chapter 27

POLITICAL EXPERIMENTS OF THE 1920s

COMMENTARY

If the foundations of today's world were laid down in World War 1, then the 1920s can be viewed as the time of attempting to build the first floor. The Peace of Paris, although intended to bring stability and trust to a war weary Europe, turned out to be cement that never dried. Instead of security each of the war's participants had complaints. Germany had been embarrassed, and the reparations demands led to endless disputes. The newly established eastern European states could not accept their newly created boundaries. As it turned out, the architects could not agree, causing demand for frequent renovations. So disturbed was the European world after the war that the efforts at stabilization and reorganization were often met with skepticism and outright violence. The political experiments of the 1920s were wide ranging and drew upon ideas from many of the theorists of the prewar era. Yet never before had governments become so much a part of their citizens' lives. World War I had caused massive centralization and control within the belligerent countries, a process that was to continue in peacetime. Considerable shifts in the sociological landscape also followed in the wake of war. Each country looked to a variety of approaches in an attempt to combine prewar ideas with the new forces generated by the war. The successes and failures of this postwar decade, like those of other historic eras, were affected by the leaders who shaped the new social, economic, and political world. Accompanying the postwar European financial, and its related social, unrest was the reality of the growing international competition from the United States and Japan.

Russia, as we have seen, had not even made it through the war. In 1917 a series of uprisings led to the Bolshevik success at the end of the year. In the following years, Lenin and his successors ruthlessly installed a wholly new socialist and totalitarian order. Though initially challenged by many groups, the Bolsheviks, aided by Leon Trotsky's genius, won out. By 1921 Lenin's New Economic Policy (NEP) promised to restore economic stability to Russia. With Lenin's death and the subsequent power struggle that followed, Josef Stalin was eventually able to establish his own permanent dictatorship. Despite the massive brutality involved, Stalin inaugurated a system that came to dominate Soviet political and economic thought into the last quarter of this century. As you will read in Chapter 30, the system built by Stalin since the late 1920's would be installed throughout eastern Europe at the end of World War II. Ultimately, "Stalinism" remains a phrase associated with extremely repressive dictators and unfortunately, in that sense, continues to affect world consciousness.

In Italy the 1920s took a different turn. Though on the victorious side, Italy was angered by the terms of the Versailles agreements because Italian territorial ambitions were thwarted. This factor, coupled with the severe internal disruptions caused by the war, brought the collapse of the parliamentary system there in 1922. In that year Benito Mussolini and the Fascists seized power. Though within a framework of legality, the Fascists were soon entrenched at all levels of government, and Mussolini assumed dictatorial control. His settlement with the church and his ability apparently to satisfy large sectors of the populace added to his strength and influence. The first fascist state would soon be ready for active and ultimately disruptive foreign adventures in the 1930s.

For both France and Great Britain the sweet taste of victory became bitter early after the war. The long struggle had disrupted many of those nations' economic enterprises and opened new avenues for political expression. The problems were more acute in France because that nation became the guardian of the Versailles Treaty. France's desire for security clouded much of her home life. The disillusionment, by 1923, sent French armies into the German Ruhr to force reparations payment. The German resistance, though passive, further aggravated the situation. For France, as for the rest of Europe, these were not easy times; but France's governments, like those of Great Britain, however frequently changed, still maintained control.

For Poland and the so-called successor states of the once Austro-Hungarian monarchy (Czechoslovakia, Hungary, Romania, Yugoslavia, Austria), the newly established independence was— except for Czechoslovakia and at times Austria—an impossible situation. Sudden independence, won as the war ended, fostered serious economic dislocation and bitter nationalist quarrels over territory and boundary lines. The problem of the nationalities, never resolved by the Dual Monarchy, proved no less troublesome for the successor states.

The Weimar Republic of Germany was saddled from the outset with an economic and psychological burden that it would not fully overcome. Impressively the government struggled to satisfy the German people and the victorious allies. The Ruhr invasion proved those efforts fruitless. Yet after 1923 there were strong signs, capped by the Locarno accords in 1925, that Germany, after all, would make it back into the "establishment" of European order.

All the political experimentation witnessed in what was America's "roaring" twenties would too quickly face the test of supreme financial disorder. As the text itself notes, and you will see in the next chapter, the Great Depression which began in 1929 would soon force European peoples to choose between their pursuit of liberal principles and the very security upon which their existence, if not well-being, depended.

IDENTIFICATIONS

Identify each one of the following as used in the text. Refer to the text as necessary.

	Text Page
"normalcy"	639
Cheka	641
Kronstadt Mutiny	641
Nikolai Bukharin	643
"socialism in one country"	643
Twenty-one Conditions	643
Bands of Combat	644
Cartel des Gauches	648
Ramsay MacDonald	649
Mohandas Gandhi	649
Sinn Fein	650
Josef Pilsudski	651
Thomas Masaryk	651
Bela Kun	651
Engelbert Dollfuss	652
Corfu Agreement of 1927	652
General John Metaxas	652
Kapp Putsch	654
Twenty-five Points	656
Mein Kampf	656
Gustav Stresemann	656-658
Charles E. Dawes/Owen D. Young	656-658
Locarno Agreements of 1925	658

MAP EXERCISE A

Locate each of the following bodies of water:

Adriatic Sea
Aegean Sea
Sea of Azov
Baltic Sea
Black Sea
Caspian Sea

Ionian Sea
Ligurian Sea
Mediterranean Sea
North Sea
the Skagerrak
Tyrrhenian Sea

Fill in or mark those countries that were created by circumstances occurring at the end of World War I.

MAP EXERCISE B

Mark the following cities and geographic points on this map of Russia.

Kiev
Moscow
Novgorod
St. Petersburg
Vladisvostok
Yakutsk

Ural Mountains
Sakhalin Island
Siberia
Lake Baikal
Bering Sea
Aral Sea

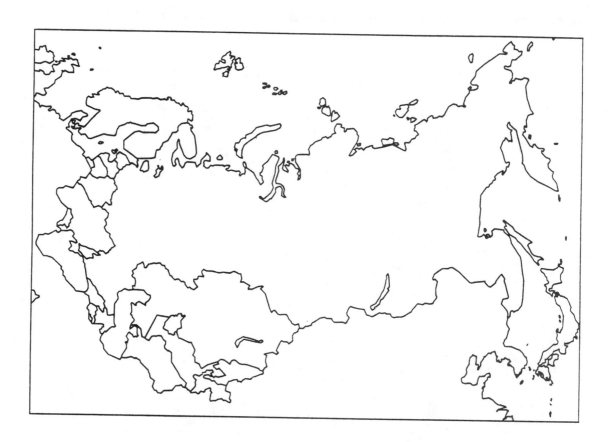

SHORT-ANSWER EXERCISES

Multiple-Choice

_____ 1. Attempts to revise the Treaty of Versailles normally stemmed from such problems as: (a) nationalistic concerns, (b) inadequate enforcement of the Treaty, (c) demands for greater self-determination in eastern Europe, (d) all of these.

_____ 2. One of the most significant social changes brought on by the war was the elevated position of particularly: (a) the elderly, (b) disabled veterans, (c) labor unions, (d) all of these.

_____ 3. Lenin's New Economic Policy permitted: (a) an open grain market, (b) private control of banking, (c) state control of every aspect of the Russian economy, (d) all of these.

_____ 4. Stalin's strength seems to have been derived from the fact that he was: (a) a master of administrative methods, (b) an excellent writer, (c) a gifted speaker, (d) witty and flashy.

_____ 5. Which of the following is the most correct statement about Mussolini: (a) he was always a nationalist, (b) he was always a socialist, (c) he originally was a socialist and became a nationalist during World War I, (d) he always put the nation before himself.

_____ 6. In the post World War I era military connections were initiated between Germany and the Soviet Union as a result of the: (a) Treaty of Rapallo, (b) Kellogg-Briand Pact, (c) Locarno Agreements, (d) Rentenmark.

_____ 7. In 1918 the British electorate included: (a) men aged twenty-one and women aged twenty-five, (b) only men, (c) men aged twenty-one and women aged thirty, (d) men and women aged twenty-one.

_____ 8. In the 1920s the Irish Civil War lingered on over the issue of: (a) the six counties of Ulster, (b) the oath of allegiance to the monarchy, (c) Protestants within the Irish Free State, (d) neutrality in world affairs.

_____ 9. All of the following opposed the Weimar Republic except: (a) army officers, (b) women, (c) judges, (d) civil servants.

_____ 10. The original appeal of the Nazi party appears to have been to: (a) the wealthy, (b) war veterans, (c) the communists, (d) Jews.

True-False

_____ 1. In the spirit of political experimentation after the First World War most countries attempted several democratic forms of government and then turned to authoritarianism.

_____ 2. Compared to the other ideologies of this era Russian communists believed that Marxism-Leninism could be established throughout the world.

_____ 3. After the stringent economic policies of "War Communism" Lenin somewhat reversed his position with his sponsorship of the New Economic Policy.

_____ 4. Josef Stalin advocated the policy of "socialism in one country."

_____ 5. The 1923 French occupation of the Ruhr industrial complex was a great success.

_____ 6. Bela Kun, Miklos Horthy, Joseph Pilsudski and Kurt von Schuschnigg are all associated with the turbulent politics of Hungary during the post-war era.

_____ 7. The actual reparations "bill" presented to Germany by the Allies in 1921 amounted to 132 million gold marks.

_____ 8.   By 1922 Hitler and the Nazi's were defining socialism along traditional German ideological lines.

_____ 9.   The election of Paul von Hindenburg to the presidency in 1925 suggests an accommodation of conservative elements to the reality of the Weimar Republic.

_____ 10.   The overall results of the many political experiments of the 1920's should be characterized as mixed at best.

Completion

1.   The idea of the necessity of communist revolutions throughout the world would be associated with the name of _____.

2.   The general term of _____ is often used to describe the right-wing dictatorships that came into being before World War II.

3.   _____ was the king of Italy from 1900 to 1946.

4.   A sensational example of Mussolini's willingness to use force and violence appears in the murder of _____.

5.   Mussolini's settlement with the Roman Catholic Church in 1929 was known as the _____.

6.   The General Strike of 1926 in Great Britain began when _____ went out on strike.

7.   During World War I the only national group to rise violently against a government was the _____.

8.   The only government carved out of the collapsed Austro-Hungarian Empire to avoid a form of authoritarian government after World War I was _____.

9.   During the Ruhr crisis of 1923 the American dollar was worth _____ German marks.

10.   As a result of the agreements at _____ a new atmosphere of hope and optimism appeared throughout Europe.

1. The struggle for power between Leon Trotsky and Josef Stalin has long been a subject for study by students of Communist Russia. What were the chief issues that divided these two men? Can you envision other factors that may have entered into the struggle?

2. Describe the manner of the Fascist takeover in Italy in 1922. What were the historic forces operating that brought Mussolini to power? How would you assess Mussolini's abilities as a politician?

3. With attention to specific problems, compare and contrast the postwar situation in Great Britain and in France.

4. Compare and contrast the inter-war development of Poland, Hungary, Czechoslovakia (now the Czech Republic and Slovakia), and what is today the former Yugoslavia?

5. Using the points noted on p. 656 of the textbook (from the Nazi Party's Twenty-five Points) comment on the political, social and economic implications of each.

Answers

Multiple-Choice

		Text Page
1.	D	639
2.	C	640
3.	A	642
4.	A	642-643
5.	C	644
6.	A	648
7.	C	648
8.	B	650
9.	B	653
10.	B	656

True-False

1.	F	639
2.	T	641
3.	T	642
4.	T	643
5.	F	648
6.	F	651-652
7.	T	654
8.	F	656
9.	T	657
10.	T	658

Completion

1.	Leon Trotsky	642
2.	*fascist*	644
3.	Victor Emmanuel III	646
4	Giacomo Matteotti	647
5	Lateran Accord	647
6.	coal miners	649
7.	Irish	650
8.	Czechoslovakia	651
9.	800 million	654
10.	Locarno	658

Chapter 28

EUROPE AND THE GREAT DEPRESSION OF THE 1930S

COMMENTARY

The worldwide difficulties caused by the Depression, which began in 1929, cannot be fully appreciated. In reality it was the first time that modern era governments had to face the economic dislocations associated with near "total" war. The period of the 1920s and 1930s was the most serious disruption in European economic life since the advent of industrialization. Unemployment—as one-time soldiers flooded the postwar labor market, faltering factory output—as industry was converted to peacetime production, severe fluctuation of the European financial structure—as the question of reparations remained unresolved, and essentially unpaid—were among the important consequences of World War I. Further compounded by national ambition and self-righteousness in the postwar era, these problems remained and by 1929 manifested themselves in the Great Depression. As time passed it was clear that the staggering cost of the war could not be borne by Germany through the ill-fated system of reparation payments. Yet France insisted on payment. Despite the problems, however, by the mid-1920s there was room for mild optimism. A reduction of reparation payment schedules and a growing atmosphere of trust, which was associated with the Locarno Conference in 1925, suggested that the "war" was finally over. The widespread development of new products like the radio and the automobile, coupled with new technological developments in synthetic production, further supported the optimistic mood.

But in the end the fragile economy of the West crashed. The largely unregulated speculation on America's stock exchanges created a ripple effect throughout the world's economy. Country after country would be forced to deal with the new circumstances created by the Great Depression.

Every nation of Europe, and the United States, was seriously affected. To this economic downturn every citizen, in one way or another, had to adjust his or her life. In all countries that were still democratic, assaults were being made on the parliamentary system of government. The totalitarian states—Germany, Russia, and Italy—were equally affected. Russia and Italy, however, had established systems of government that could go well beyond the normal restrictions imposed by the democracies, and Germany was in the process of doing so. In some cases organized and violent control over the citizenry allowed those countries to weather the economic crisis of the Depression. Their success was sometimes viewed as positive proof that totalitarianism was the future form of government for all of Europe.

Great Britain and France managed to survive by accepting political coalitions and economic ideas not dreamed of in the pre-war era. Italy's Mussolini never fully solved the problem of economic needs in his country and by 1935 resorted to international adventures to take pressure off Fascist failings at home.

Germany, the most severely struck by the Depression, fell into the grasp of Hitler and the Nazis, who never failed to brutally eliminate opponents, real or imagined. No one person, no group, not even an entire race of people could be secure against this open and organized assault on humanity witnessed during the Nazi era.

Although the facts are less visible in the U.S.S.R., there is little doubt that the vast economic reorganization of Russia instituted by Stalin caused an untold hardship on Soviet citizens. The industrial machine created by the Five Year Plans, and admired by many in the West, was oiled by the blood of millions. It is clear today that even with the passing of the Soviet Union as an economic entity, Russia's economic problems remain serious and deeply rooted. The economic hardships suffered by the Russian populace under the Czars and under communism continue to defy simple and quick solutions. And this regardless of western aid and the concomitant encouragement of capitalist style approaches there.

As a catastrophe of the Western world, the Great Depression taught many hard lessons. But before these could be fully realized, Europe had been pushed into World War II.

IDENTIFICATIONS

Identify each one of the following as used in the text. Refer to text as necessary.

	Text Page
Keynesian economic theory	644
ad valorem tariff	666
Croix de Feu	666
Leon Blum	667
Paul von Hindenburg	668-669
Franz von Papen	669
Article 48 of the Weimar Constitution	670
Enabling Act Of 1933	670
Ernst Roehm	670
Schutzstaffel	670
Kristallnacht	671
Nazi Four-Year Plan	671
corporatism	673
Gosplan	674
kulaks	675-676
Sergei Kirov	677
"old Bolsheviks"	677

MAP EXERCISE A

On the accompanying map, shade the areas of the world controlled by dictatorships in 1939:

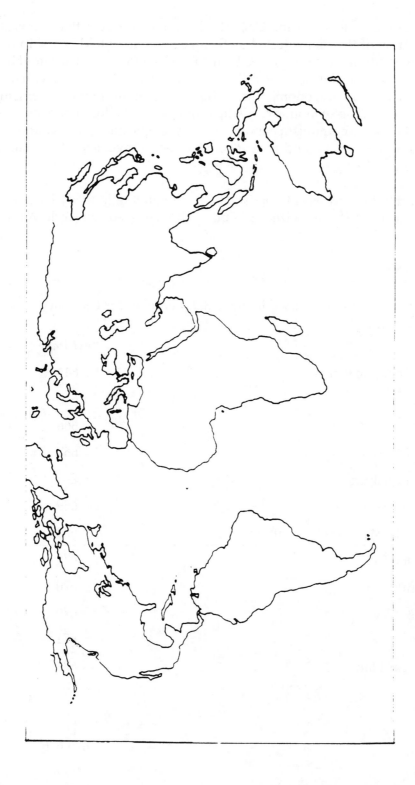

MAP EXERCISE B

On this map of the European continent mark all of the countries of Europe with the approximate boundaries of 1939.

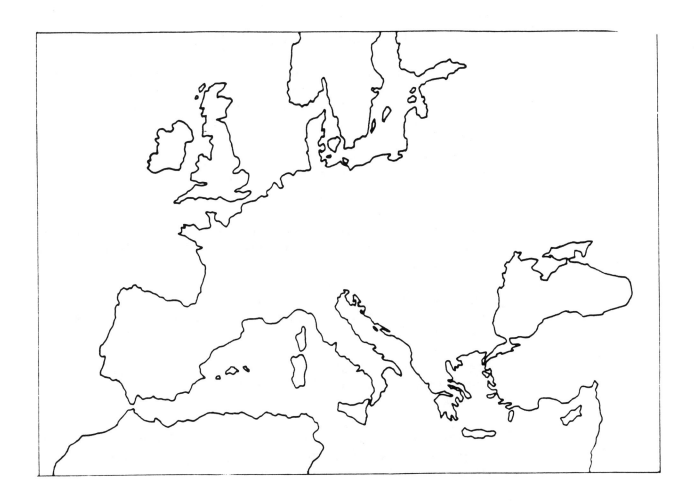

SHORT-ANSWER EXERCISES

Multiple-Choice

_____ 1. The world commodity market of the 1930s saw: (a) food production surpass demand, (b) government-accumulated reserves at record levels, (c) the price of foodstuffs drop severely, (d) all of these.

_____ 2. Which of the following British Prime Ministers is most noted for coming to grips with the economic problems stemming from the Great Depression: (a) Stanley Baldwin, (b) Winston Churchill, (c) Neville Chamberlain, (d) Ramsay MacDonald.

_____ 3. Right-wing groups in France such as the *Action Française* and the *Croix de Feu* were opposed to all of the following except: (a) military rule, (b) socialism, (c) communism, (d) parliamentary rule.

_____ 4. The country that actually suffered from the greatest unemployment problem in the late 1920s and the early 1930s was (a) Germany, (b) Italy, (c) France, (d) Great Britain.

_____ 5. By the 1930s the least likely support for the Nazi party within Germany came from: (a) the young, (b) communists, (c) most intellectuals, (d) war veterans.

_____ 6. The widespread 1938 attack upon Jewish stores and synagogues throughout Germany is known as: (a) the Final Solution, (b) Nazi Day, (c) *Kristallnacht*, (d) Nuremberg Law Day.

_____ 7. Which of the following was not a part of Mussolini's economic program: (a) importation of foreign grain supplies, (b) vast public works programs, (c) protective tariffs, (d) subsidies to industries.

_____ 8. Between the years 1928 and 1940 Soviet industrial growth appears to have been near: (a) 100 percent, (b) 400 percent, (c) 200 percent, (d) 50 percent.

_____ 9. "Dizziness from success," is a phrase ascribed to: (a) Benito Mussolini, (b) Franklin Roosevelt, (c) Joseph Stalin, (d) the Beatles.

_____ 10. Which of the following events occurred first: (a) Hindenburg defeats Hitler for the presidency of Germany, (b) New York stock market collapses, (c) assassination of Sergei Kirov, (d) Reichstag fire.

True-False

_____ 1. Disruption in the world marketplace and the financial crisis caused by the First World War led to the Great Depression.

_____ 2. In the years immediately after the war it was the United States that insisted upon repayment of war debts.

_____ 3. The idea of increasing government spending to offset the effects of the Depression is normally associated with British Prime Minister Ramsay MacDonald.

_____ 4. By 1934 Great Britain was exceeding her pre-Depression level of production.

_____ 5. Léon Blum's leadership of the French Popular Front aimed at establishing a socialist and democratic government.

_____ 6. In the 1932 *Reichstag* elections saw the Nazi party gain a clear parliamentary majority.

_____ 7. Anti-Semitism became a key element of the Nazi program in Germany only after Hitler gained power in 1933.

_____ 8. Lenin's New Economic Policy firmly established the economic program of communism in the Soviet Union.

_____ 9. The State Planning Commission (Gosplan) had the overall responsibility for industrial planning in the Soviet Union.

_____ 10. The best estimate for the number of people executed and imprisoned as a result of Stalin's purges is in the hundreds of thousands.

Completion

1. The 1931 moratorium on all international debt was initiated by the American President _____.

2. _____ wrote the *General Theory of Employment, Interest, and Money.*

3. In 1931 a British political coalition of Labor, Conservative, and Liberal ministers formed the so-called _____.

4. Rule by emergency decree was permitted under Article number _____ of the Weimar Constitution.

5. After the incident of the _____ the German *Reichstag* allowed Hitler to rule by decree.

6. As a result of the death of _____ Hitler was able to combine the offices of chancellor and president into one.

7. By 1936 _____ was in charge of all police functions in Germany.

8. _____ was the 1935 series of laws passed against German Jews and their institutions.

9. _____ was the country invaded by Italy in 1935.

10. _____ is the word used to describe the agricultural reorganization of Russia under Stalin.

FOR FURTHER CONSIDERATION

1. Describe the politics surrounding and the reform policies of Leon Blum and the Popular Front in France.

2. In an examination of German political maneuvering between 1930 and Hitler's appointment as Chancellor in 1933, what factors, beyond the clearly economic, seem to have undermined the Weimar Republic?

3. Using both Italian and German examples describe the economic system of fascism, or corporatism. Generally, what was the fascist view of private property and of capital?

4. Describe the causes, aims, and effects of the Stalinist purges.

5. In your opinion why were the ruthless policies of the dictatorships of the 1930s possible? Why were they so often successful?

ANSWERS

Multiple-Choice

		Text Page
1.	D	663-664
2.	D	665
3.	A	666
4.	A	668
5.	B	668
6.	C	671
7.	A	673
8.	B	674
9.	C	676
10	B	*passim*

True-False

1.	T	662
2.	T	663
3.	F	664
4.	T	666
5.	T	667
6.	F	669
7.	F	671
8.	F	674
9.	T	674
10.	F	676

Completion

1.	Herbert Hoover	663
2.	John Maynard Keynes	664
3.	National Government	665
4.	48	668
5.	Reichstag Fire	670
6.	President Hindenburg	670
7.	Heinrich Himmler	670
8.	Nuremberg Laws	671
9.	Ethiopia	673
10.	collectivization	675-676

WORLD WAR II

COMMENTARY

The answers to complex historical questions and/or situations are never easy to assess. This most certainly is true of the wars of this century. They are close to us in time, and continue to effect the world in which we live. The roots of World War I were embedded in the nineteenth century and earlier; those of World War II lie there as well and in the events surrounding the 1914-1918 war. Unquestionably the Great Depression was a factor that further fostered circumstances and decisions not contemplated in an earlier era. However, the normal historical evaluation of the origins of World War II are made even more difficult by at least two other factors. Both reflect the inescapable problem of human life in general and the contemporary nature of the event which ended just over fifty years ago. First, the Nazi racial program of mass extermination of many different peoples and the outright genocide against European Jews is one nearly incomprehensible factor, almost defying explanation. Second, in our own time we continue to experience problems relating to the war, to the succeeding Cold War, and now post-Cold War conditions.

It is clear that conditions in Europe between the wars coupled with aggressive totalitarian nationalism were major causes of the war. Real and perceived injustices, the collapse of the concept of collective security, uncertain, and often indecisive national policies represent additional factors. However broad these characteristics of the inter-war years may appear to us, the road to World War II has a deliberate direction. Without question the Weimar Republic was the most strained by the world war that ended in 1918. Awakened nationalism and heightened socioeconomic problems were parleyed by the Nazi Party into complete control of Germany. Becoming Chancellor in 1933 Adolf Hitler was in a position to bring his ideas and former pronouncements into being. By the early 1930s the post war hope for a peace sponsored by the newly formed League of Nations collapsed as Japan invaded Manchuria (1931), and Italy attacked Ethiopia (1935). A crucial test for France came in March 1936 when German troops re-occupied the Rhineland in deliberate violation of the Versailles Treaty and the Locarno Pacts of 1925. The failure to act against this blatant disregard for solemn agreements only increased the appetite of the augmentative dictators. Hitler and Mussolini supported the rebels in Spain which allowed a fascist government under General Francisco Franco to emerge there in 1939. The Nazi's brought increasing pressures against Austria and Czechoslovakia. A near-war in the spring of 1938 over the Sudetenland of Czechoslovakia set the stage for the effective destruction of the most successful of the central European states created at the end of World War I. The Munich Conference averted immediate war, but emboldened Hitler and left England and France apparently cowered, and sent Italy further into Hitler's embrace. In a surprise move the communist state of the Soviet Union and the fascist state of Germany became strange bedfellows indeed, by signing the Nazi-Soviet Pact of 1939, sealing Poland's fate.

Chapter 29

World War II was on. For the first time in human history war was truly global. Destruction raged across three continents (Europe, Asia, and Africa) and over and under vast oceans. From the invasion of Poland in September, 1939 to the collapse of France in the summer of 1941 the Germans experienced complete success in their military conquests. But Churchill's Britain would not yield. The German air attack there proved futile, while Hitler's support of Mussolini's faltering legions in Africa and the Balkans delayed the massive assault into Russia. By the end of 1941 two significant factors were beginning to operate. The German offensive in Russia had been stopped before Moscow changing the character of the war in the east, and Imperial Japan launched a surprise air attack against American ships and naval facilities at Hawaii quickly bringing the United States into World War II. By 1943, though far from over, and with Italy out of the picture, the war's direction was being governed by the Allies. Russian pressures in the east and the Normandy invasion in mid-1944 put the Germans almost totally on the defensive. By May, 1945 with the war over in Europe, two nuclear attacks on their cities brought Japan's formal surrender in September of that year. The Second "Great" War of this century was over, and with it European domination of the planet came to an end.

Exemplified by a wartime series of head-of-state "summit-type" meetings, the mutual distrust of the Western democracies and communist Russia was only temporarily suspended, and never totally. In the power vacuum thus created the U.S. (United States) and the former S.U. (Union of Soviet Socialist Republics) moved from a reluctant partnership of the wartime era to being global adversaries shortly after the war concluded.

It is this post World War II juxtaposition of global power that emerged as the dominant factor of the last half century and molded the contemporary posture of the western state system. Remarkably, as the early 1990s has already shown, the world created out of the ruins of World War II is changing dramatically in a direction no one could at this moment predict.

Today it is even clearer, as more once-secret information becomes available, that the tension of Cold War politics started before the bombs stopped falling. It is this Cold War that has effectively dominated the scene since the end of World War II. Much controversy surrounds the origins of the Cold War.

Unclear intentions, expansionist motives, growing mistrust, and Stalinist support of communist parties in eastern Europe have all contributed to the post World War II atmosphere. The end of the war left too many unresolved international and colonial problems for the infant United Nations to deal with. Too much physical and psychological damage, too much an upset to established order, too much tension had developed for any easy solution. With much less notice at the time the world had passed into the nuclear age. The nations of the world and those peoples seeking nationhood in the wake of the Second World War faced too many uncertainties after 1945—uncertainties that are now a part of the contemporary Western heritage.

Identify each one of the following as used in the text. Refer to the text as necessary.

	Text Page
Lebensraum	681
Lytton Report	681
Stresa Front	681
Rome-Berlin "Axis"	682
Anschluss	683
Konrad Henlein	683
Neville Chamberlain	684
Nazi-Soviet nonaggression pact	685
"Blitzkrieg"	685
Maginot Line	686
Operation Barbarossa	687
Hitler's "new order"	689
Albert Speer	698
Josef Goebbels	699
Vichy France	699
Charles de Gaulle	699-700
Lord Beaverbrook	700
Atlantic Charter	702
"Big Three"	702
Clement Attlee	704
Oder-Niesse River Line	704

MAP EXERCISE A

1. Outline the area known as the Sudetenland of Czechoslovakia.
2. Draw a line showing the areas of concentration of Czech and Slovak peoples.
3. Locate the city of Prague on the map.
4. Locate Poland; show the so-called "Polish Corridor" dividing Germany in 1939.
5. Locate the Baltic states of Latvia, Estonia, Lithuania, and Finland.
6. Locate each of the following cities: Berlin, Warsaw, Danzig, and Helsinki.

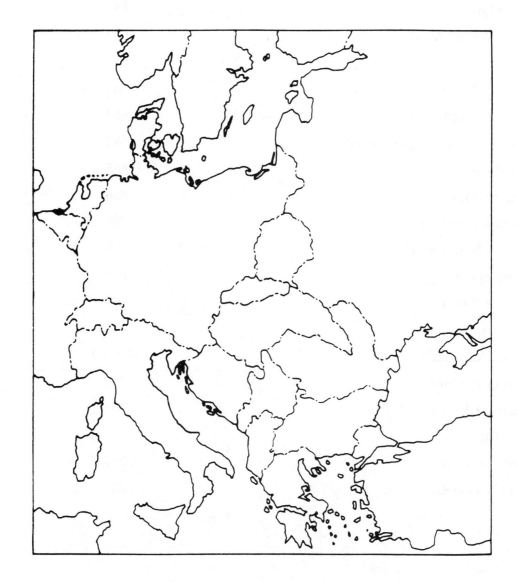

MAP EXERCISE B

On this world map mark the major battle lines/fronts and battles of World War II on land and at sea.

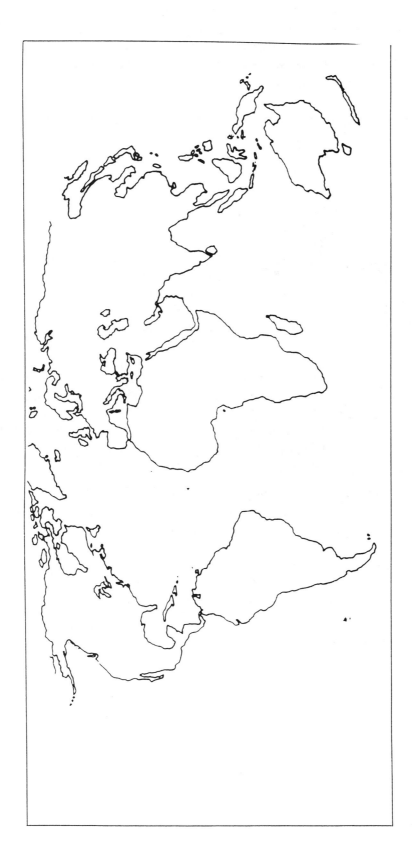

SHORT-ANSWER EXERCISES

Multiple-Choice

_____ 1. Which of the following represents the best explanation for the 1935 Italian invasion of Ethiopia: (a) to divert attention from economic conditions in Italy, (b) the need to avenge the Italian defeat there in 1896, (c) the desire to restore the glory of ancient Rome, (d) all of these.

_____ 2. The establishment of the Spanish Republic in 1931 brought to power a government that supported: (a) the Catholic Church, (b) separatists and radicals, (c) large landowners, (d) none of these.

_____ 3. After the Munich Conference: (a) Benito Mussolini, (b) Neville Chamberlain, (c) Konrad Henlein, (d) Adolf Hitler, renounced further territorial demands in Europe.

_____ 4. (a) His ability as a writer and speaker, (b) his confidence in Britain, (c) his attitude toward British nationalism, (d) all of these, contributed to Winston Churchill's success as a British leader.

_____ 5. German racial policies were least applied in: (a) Norway, (b) Russia, (c) Poland, (d) the Slavic countries in general.

_____ 6. (a) Italy, (b) Soviet Union, (c) Hungary, (d) Romania, would be considered along with Nazi Germany as unmatched in the committing of atrocities.

_____ 7. The 1945 "Battle of the Bulge" had the effect of showing that: (a) Germany would soon lose the war, (b) years of tough fighting might possibly lie ahead, (c) Japan was finished, (d) American soldiers were no match for the Germans.

_____ 8. Which of the following statements best describes the reasons behind the decision to use the atomic bomb: (a) it was unnecessary to win the war, but it would teach the yellow races a lesson, (b) the use of the bomb by the United States would make the Russians more cooperative after the war, (c) it was a way to end the war and save American lives, (d) the decision was not thought out at all.

_____ 9. During World War II German women were: (a) portrayed as docile helpmates, (b) forbidden to have sexual relations with non-Germans, (c) not allowed to work in munitions factories, (d) only permitted agriculturally related jobs.

_____ 10. The most important military decision at the 1943 Tehran Conference involved: (a) Russia's promises to attack Japan, (b) an allied offensive in the Balkans, (c) establishment of a United Nations' army, (d) an offensive on Europe's west coast.

True-False

_____ 1. Falangists were members of the pro-fascist parties opposing the Spanish Popular Front government in the Civil War there.

_____ 2. After signing the Munich agreements in September 1938, Hitler believed that it was "peace with honor."

_____ 3. The 1939 Nazi-Soviet Pact secretly divided Poland between Germany and the Soviet Union.

_____ 4. The French government which accepted defeat at the hands of the Germans ironically was led by a former World War I military hero.

_____ 5. Fighting in North Africa against both the British and later the Americans earned German General Erwin Rommel the accolade of "The Desert Fox."

_____ 6. In late 1941 General Tojo led the Japanese militarists toward war with the United States.

_____ 7. "Island hopping" was a popular dance craze during the 1940s.

_____ 8. That Japan could keep Hirohito as emperor was the only condition under which Japan surrendered to the United States in August of 1945.

_____ 9. In general, Vichy France tended toward liberal excesses.

_____ 10. Routine bombing of civilians during World War II was successful in demoralizing the home fronts.

Completion

1. *Lebensraum* required the conquest of _______________ and the _______________.

2. Haunted by the _______________ of the last war, neither Great Britain nor France was willing to respond to Hitler's earlier provocations.

3. In 1936 General _______________ led the revolt against the Spanish Popular Front.

4. In the late 1930s many of Adolf Hitler's gains came as a result of the British Prime Minister Neville Chamberlain's policy of _______________.

5. Within Nazi Germany's racial theory the Slavic peoples were considered subhuman creatures known in German as _______________.

6. The German word _______________ means "purified of Jews."

7. The first reversal of Axis progress in World War II came with the American naval victories in the battles of _______________ and _______________.

8. The turning point of the Russian campaign came with the battle of _______________ during the winter of 1942-1943.

9. The first meeting of the wartime allies (Churchill, Roosevelt, and Stalin) took place in _____.

10. _____ was the only representative of the three major victorious powers who could attend both the Yalta and Potsdam Conferences.

FOR FURTHER CONSIDERATION

1. Discuss the Munich Agreement of 1938. Outline the position of the states directly involved. Does this settlement contain any lessons for the contemporary world?

2. Discuss the questions surrounding high-altitude bombing during World War II. What were the primary and secondary targets? Was this method effective? Do the lessons learned in precision bombing during World War II have any effect on us today?

3. Suppose that the Nazis had not adopted the racial policies that they did. In your opinion, would the outcome of World War II have been any different? If the outcome had been the same, how might historians have come to judge the rise and fall of Adolf Hitler?

4. Considering the respective backgrounds of World War I and World War II, compare and contrast the founding of the League of Nations with the founding of the United Nations.

5. Discuss Stalin's policies and leadership throughout this period? In your opinion was Russia's position respective to the rise of Nazism equally responsible for the war? Answer with specific details as needed.

ANSWERS

Multiple-Choice

		Text Page
1.	D	681-682
2.	D	683
3.	D	684
4.	D	686
5.	A	689
6.	B	691
7.	A	696
8.	C	697
9.	B	698-699
10.	D	702

True-False

1.	T	683
2.	F	684
3.	T	685
4.	T	686
5.	T	687
6.	T	692
7.	F	696
8.	T	696
9.	F	699
10.	F	700

Completion

1.	Poland/Ukraine	681
2.	memories	682
3.	Francisco Franco	683
4.	appeasement	684
5.	*untermenschen*	689
6.	*Judenrein*	690
7.	Coral Sea/Midway Island	693
8.	Stalingrad	693
9.	Tehran, Iran	702
10.	Josef Stalin	703-704

EUROPE AND THE SOVIET-AMERICAN RIVALRY

COMMENTARY

Today it is even clearer, as more once secret information becomes available, that the tension of Cold War politics actually started before the bombs stopped falling in World War II. It was this "Cold War" that effectively dominated most global events at least into the 1970s. The current trend is to accept that this Cold War which had so long fashioned international competition between the United States and the Soviet Union has ended. However, be mindful that much controversy surrounds the origins and direction of this postwar condition. Unclear intentions, expansionist motives, growing mistrust, and Stalinist support of communist parties in eastern Europe; and corresponding support by the United States for democratic (anti-communist) governments in western Europe, all contributed to the strained atmosphere of those first decades after World War II. United States sponsored initiatives for the end of European controls over vast areas of Asia and Africa further complicated the scene after World War II. With victory U.S. trade and commerce, supported by sustained economic growth during and after the war, was soon global in character and influence. The Europeanization of the world that had started in the last century rapidly became, at least into the 1980s, a period of "Americanization."

The end of the war left too many unresolved international and colonial problems for the infant United Nations to deal with. That international organization, the successor of the League of Nations, despite all good intentions, was not able to positively influence the international and regional rivalries wrought by the war. The end of World War II left too much physical and psychological damage, too much of an upset to established order, and too much international tension for easy or cooperative solutions.

In the summer of 1945 the world, as a result of the United States development and utilization of atomic bombs to end the war in Asia, passed into the nuclear age.

Contemporaneously, the nations of the world and those peoples seeking nationhood in the wake of World War II faced many uncertainties and a compelling need to rebuild. They had to reconstruct physical damage and needed to reevaluate and reorganize their sense of national and regional destiny. This process has continued into the present era against a backdrop of the Cold War, decolonization in Africa and Asia, and international uncertainty. Within this broad context intermittent strategic arms talks between the U.S. and the S.U. often have been viewed as a key barometer of East-West relations.

In the last decade there has been a relaxation of tension between the superpowers; but this seeming calm from time to time has been punctuated by regional crises.

However, in the period immediately following the War's end Soviet expansionism in Europe and the establishment of communist government in China were catalysts for the "containment" policy fostered by the United States. Fear of the spread of communism across the ruins of Europe and Asia nurtured American programs such as the Truman Doctrine and the Marshall Plan. Narrowly averting war in Germany in 1948, the Cold War heated up on the Korean Peninsula when a Russian supported communist North Korea invaded South Korea. A military stalemate there coupled with Stalin's death and a new American president (Eisenhower) brought a cease fire in 1953.

Without question World War II precipitated and in some instances hastened the withdrawal of European states from their former colonial territories. The process was rarely a smooth one, and residual bitterness remains. When Great Britain pulled out of the Indian sub-continent several rival states were necessarily formed along religious lines. The transition to independence in Africa has rarely been without bloodshed. Here in the 1990's there is continued evidence of bitter tribal struggles that threaten to take man's inhumanity to new heights. Decolonization for their former colonies in Indo-China was painfully resisted by the French, and ultimately drew the United States into the region in a Cold War struggle against communism in Vietnam. Only now are U.S.-Vietnamese relations showing signs of what might be approaching normalcy.

The growing American military and economic support commitment to South Vietnam brought on considerable domestic protest. These "peace" movements joined a confluence of civil and gender rights movements that had appeared after World War II. In reality, the modern civil rights movement grew out of the "Double Victory" campaign organized by African-American leaders during the early 1940's in support of the war effort and their own political agenda to gain racial equality. Re-stimulated by the Truman administration's integration of the armed forces and the 1954 *Brown* decision the movement gained support beyond the confines of the black community. Martin Luther King, Jr., until his murder in 1968, was most closely associated with the civil rights activism and successes during this era.

The bold initiatives of the Reagan-Bush presidencies, such as the Strategic Defense Initiative and the American supported United Nations defense of Kuwait, effectively ended the Cold War era and with growing uncertainties ushered in an era of collective security in which the United Nations is poised to play an important role.

Although less is known of the Soviet side of things, the end of the Korean conflict coupled to Stalin's death in 1953 created a brief period of uncertainty there that ended with the emergence of Nikita Khrushchev as the new Soviet leader. His government tried to take the Soviet Union to new domestic and international heights; but very well may have started the process that eventuated the end of the Marxist-Leninist (and Stalinist) dictatorship there. In retrospect, the Cuban Missile Crisis was the most dangerous moment in the Cold War. While the threat of a nuclear holocaust loomed at the time (1962), it is only recently that the world has learned (from previously secret Soviet documents) just how close it was.

With the 1990s it seems apparent that a new world, fashioned out of the Cold War arena, is emerging. Vast changes in eastern Europe, unheard of a decade ago, are occurring with the encouragement of the now defunct Soviet Union. Stirred by the reform program of leader Gorbachev, and now under President Boris Yeltsin the former Soviet Union, reconstituted as the Commonwealth of Independent States (C.I.S.), is engaged in a major restructuring program of its entire political and economic system. Constructive political and economic change and the hoped for material progress appear as key goals in this effort.

The reunification of Germany once again is demonstrating the powerful allure of nationalist sentiment. These changes will be further examined in the concluding chapter of the text "Toward a New Europe and the Twenty-first Century."

On the one hand the collapse of Soviet control over Eastern Europe has ushered in a period of unprecedented change there. For the western states the first cautious steps toward European integration have been taken. The European Economic Community has taken on a new life in what is no longer post-war Europe.

One of the most complex and long-standing trouble spots has been in the Middle East. Here the violent admixture of Cold War politics, decolonization, and bitter religious hatred, coupled with the natural resource (oil) of the region, has created a caldron of local and regional rivalries. The abortive invasion (August 1990) of Kuwait by neighboring Iraq represents the most current example. Add to this the establishment of the state of Israel, and the subsequent wars that erupted in the region since 1948, and the Middle East, even as the Cold War wanes, must remain high on the list of potential world trouble spots. A promising era may be dawning. Whatever successes there may be in the 1990s it should be recalled that the process began in the 1970s. Anwar el-Sadat, Egypt's president from 1970 until his assassination in 1981, took the major steps toward reconciliation in the late 1970s. Supported in these efforts and ultimately moderated by U.S. President Jimmy Carter the Camp David Accords (1977) became in time a key instrument toward invoking a settlement of fundamental issues dividing Arabs and Israelis. Today, as we go to press, there are hopeful signs that old enemies can continue to work collectively and compromisingly toward a new stability in the area.

IDENTIFICATIONS

Identify each one of the following as used in the text. Refer to the text as necessary.

	Text Page
Vyacheslav Molotov	708
"iron curtain" speech	708-709
"containment" policy	710
Cominform	711
Kim Il Sung	712
General Douglas MacArthur	712
Brown vs. Board of Education, Topeka, KA	714
New Frontier and the Great Society	715
Watergate	716
Manual Noriega	717
Operation Desert Storm	717
Khrushchev's "secret speech"	718
Gamal Abdel Nasser	718-719 and 733-734
Wladyslaw Gomulka	719
"peaceful coexistence"	719
Prague Spring	721
Helsinki Accords	722
Strategic Defense Initiative	722
Lech Walesa	723
General Wojciech Jaruzelski	723
Margaret Thatcher	724
Charles de Gaulle	724
OEEC	725
Common Market	725
Treaty of Maastricht	726
Ho Chi Minh	728-730
Ngo Dinh Diem	730-731
Theodore Herzl	732
Gamal Abdel Nasser	733
Anwar el-Sadat	734
Camp David Accords	734
PLO	734-735
intifada	735

MAP EXERCISE A

(1) On the accompanying map of the Korean Peninsula locate each of the following:

1. 38th parallel
2. Seoul
3. Pyongyang
4. Chosan

5. Pusan
6. Inchon
7. Panmunjom
8. 1953 armistice line

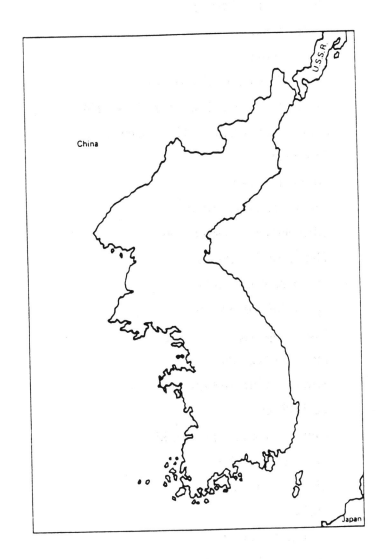

MAP EXERCISE B

(2) On the accompanying map of Southeast Asia locate each of the following:

1. Laos
2. Thailand
3. Cambodia (Khmer Republic)
4. North/South Vietnam
5. Bangkok
6. Phnom Penh
7. Saigon (Ho Chi Minh City)
8. Dien Bien Phu
9. Hanoi
10. Haiphong
11. Gulf of Tonkin
12. Hue
13. Pleiku
14. Mekong delta

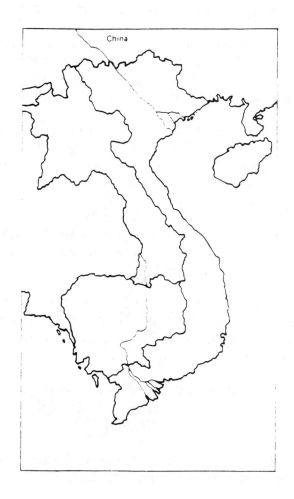

Multiple-Choice

_____ 1.   Disappointment in the early efforts of the United Nations to resolve international conflicts can be viewed as caused by: (a) the voluntary nature of the organization, (b) its inability to deal with internal problems of troublesome nations, (c) the veto power as exercised in the Security Council, (d) all of these.

_____ 2.   The Marshall Plan can be considered: (a) a complete failure, (b) only moderately successful, (c) a great success, (d) neither a success nor failure.

_____ 3.   Which of the following would not be considered among the highlights of the American Civil Rights Movement: (a) the assassination of Martin Luther King, Jr., (b) the Montgomery, Alabama Bus Boycott, (c) the 1963 "March on Washington," (d) the Voting Rights Act of 1965.

_____ 4.   Which is the correct post-World War II order for these presidents of the United States: (a) Ford, Carter, Nixon, Reagan, Bush, (b) Eisenhower, Kennedy, Johnson, Ford, Carter (c) Truman, Eisenhower, Kennedy, Bush, Reagan, (d) Johnson, Kennedy, Nixon, Ford, Reagan.

_____ 5.   Which is the correct post-World War II order for these leaders of the Soviet Union: (a) Andropov, Khrushchev, Brezhnev, Gorbachev, (b) Stalin, Khrushchev, Yeltsin, Gorbachev, (c) Chernenko, Khrushchev, Brezhnev, Andropov, (d) none of these are correct.

_____ 6.   Russian Premier Khrushchev's abrupt ending of the 1960 Summit Conference at Paris was caused mainly by: (a) an unsatisfactory settlement of the Berlin issue, (b) the Cuban Missile Crisis, (c) the U-2 incident, (d) his demand for President Eisenhower's resignation.

_____ 7.   The "most dangerous days" of the Cold War thus far are usually associated with the: (a) Korean War, (b) construction of the Berlin Wall, (c) Cuban Missile Crisis, (d) American intervention in Vietnam.

_____ 8.   (a) Alexei Kosygin, (b) Nikita Khrushchev, (c) Leonid Brezhnev, (d) Lavrenti Beria, is considered to have been the most powerful Russian leader since Stalin's era.

_____ 9.   In 1964 an attack on an American naval vessel (a) off the west coast of Korea, (b) in the Gulf of Tonkin, (c) off the coast of Cambodia, (d) off the coast of Laos, led to increased United States involvement in Vietnam.

_____ 10.   Continuous American involvement in the recent era of Middle Eastern affairs is symbolized by the: (a) Helsinki Accords, (b) Nixon Doctrine, (c) U.S. recognition of the PLO, (d) Camp David Accords.

True-False

_____ 1. In 1946 Winston Churchill delivered his famed "Iron Curtain" speech to a joint session of the Congress of the United States.

_____ 2. In enunciating the Truman Doctrine in 1947 the President implied that the United States would support free peoples against aggression everywhere in the world.

_____ 3. The concept of the "New Deal" is associated with the Truman administration.

_____ 4. Martin Luther King, Jr. advocated violence against whites in order to achieve racial equality in the United States.

_____ 5. President Richard Nixon's opening to China is probably his most important diplomatic achievement.

_____ 6. As a result of the Watergate scandal Richard Nixon resigned from the Office of the President of the United States; the second president in U.S. history to do so.

_____ 7. The Suez incident of 1956 clearly demonstrated the influence of the United States in world affairs.

_____ 8. Nationalist movements, colonial revolts, and Cold War politics are all factors in the so-called decolonization movement.

_____ 9. South Vietnamese President Diem and American President Kennedy were murdered in the same month.

_____ 10. American involvement in Southeast Asia throughout the 1960s allowed western European states to question American power and influence, and eroded the position of United States leadership of the free world.

Completion

1. Unlike its support for the _____ the United States took a leading role in the formation of the _____.

2. The attempt to deal with the problem of _____ was an early victim of the Cold War.

3. The murder of _____ was an early sign of communist intentions in eastern Europe.

4. The 1955 formation of the _____ as an eastern bloc military alliance demonstrated the extent of Cold war politics in Europe.

5. It would appear that the U. S. involvement in the early 1950s Korean conflict was interpreted by American policy makers as a success for the concept known as _____.

6. The erection of the Berlin Wall occurred during the American presidency of _____.

7. Russian novelist, _____ was one of the most prominent Soviet dissidents during the Brezhnev era.

8. The defeat of the French forces in the battle of _____ effectively ended France's involvement in Indo-China.

9. President Richard Nixon's policy aimed at the gradual withdrawal of American combat forces from Vietnam was known as _____.

10. As early as 1917 the British government in issuing the _____ favored the establishment of a Jewish homeland in Palestine.

FOR FURTHER CONSIDERATION

1. In your opinion, how did the American response to and policy development in respect to the Korean "police action" of 1950-1953 relate to later U.S. involvement in Vietnam?

2. Discuss the economic experiments sponsored under Nikita Khrushchev's leadership of the Soviet Union? Do these policies have a later effect? If so, discuss their implications in detail.

3. Describe the course of events in the post-World War II rivalry between the United States and the Soviet Union. Cite the significant examples of this superpower competition? What in your view led to the end of the Cold War?

4. What were the origins of the Indo-China conflict? Discuss the motivations of the major participants in that area's troubles over the thirty-year period beginning in 1945. Try to characterize the positions of each of the following countries: France, Russia, China, United States, South Vietnam, North Vietnam.

5. Discuss the Arab-Israeli conflict since 1948. In your view, what is the most fundamental problem in this area of conflict? How can the dispute be resolved on a permanent basis? Develop your answer fully.

Answers

Multiple-Choice

		Text Page
1.	D	710
2.	C	710
3.	A	715
4	B	*passim*
5	D	*passim*
6.	C	720
7.	C	720
8.	C	721
9.	B	731
10.	D	734

True-False

1.	F	708-709
2.	T	710
3.	F	714
4.	F	714
5.	T	716
6.	F	716
7.	T	719
8.	T	726-728
9.	T	731
10.	T	732

Completion

1.	League of Nations/United Nations	708
2.	atomic energy	710
3.	Jan Masaryk	711
4.	Warsaw Pact	712
5.	containment	713
6.	John F. Kennedy	720
7.	Aleksandr Solzhenitsyn	721
8.	Dien Bien Phu	730
9.	*Vietnamization*	732
10.	Balfour Declaration	732

For Further Consideration of the Documents

Each of the following questions is designed to help you reach a better understanding of certain of the original documents presented in the last five chapters of the text. Feel free to use the page numbers provided to refer back to the document as necessary. The value of a primary historical source should not be underestimated; it helps us understand the nature of the era in which it was written.

The French Minister on the Russian Revolution (pp. 628-629)
1. Place yourself at the scene. Was Ambassador Paleologue's reminder of Charles X's position in 1830 and Louis Philippe's in 1848 valid? Explain.

Hitler on the Versailles Treaty (pp. 654-655)
2. Place yourself in the audience. What are the arguments advanced by the future dictator of Germany? Are they valid in your opinion? What does Hitler advance as the basic demands of his party?

A Woman in the Slums (p. 665)
3. Define poverty? Using a real or imagined example describe a situation today such as George Orwell did in the 1930s.

Extermination at Belsen (p. 690-691)
4. How do you react to this description? What reasons can you find for the lack of apparent resistance to these horrors by the victims themselves?

Churchill's Iron Curtain (p. 709)
5. The western policy toward the Soviet Union in the late 1940s was defined in part by this speech. List exactly what the communists/Russians were accused of. Explain as necessary.

TOWARD A NEW EUROPE AND THE TWENTY-FIRST CENTURY

COMMENTARY

This concluding chapter reviews a number of major trends which continue to influence the world as we know it. Certainly the expanded and increasingly influential role that women are playing in modern societies will remain a central element in most societies for the foreseeable future. This new, essentially post-World War II role of women has effected the way the work place operates, and the way children are raised in Western societies. It has altered, and some would argue detrimentally, the family. Future decades will undoubtedly see a greater sharing of all job and familial responsibilities between the sexes.

Women are also participating in university education as never before. Clearly, the student experience, once limited to a relatively small, elite, male group in Western society has broadened to include a much wider cross-section of European and American societies. Although the 1960's are considered the high point of student activism, today's students are involved in a number of political, environmental, and social issues. They have become part of the flow of information that has dramatically accelerated more than in any previous era. Current intellectual trends continue to develop within an ever-widening diffusion of knowledge. Dramatic growth of what might be called the "intellectual or university community" has brought vast areas of scientific and humanistic learning to a growing number of persons and social groups as never before. Students from all social and economic classes travel as never before. Student culture is further supported by trends in "pop" music with rock remaining a constant. The authors assert that rock music with its emphasis on free expression, community and peace was a factor in the collapse of authoritarianism in eastern Europe in the early 1990's.

Within Western civilization, as well as the rest of the world, there is a current information explosion that shows every sign of continued growth. This electronically generated revolution should not be underestimated as it contains the means for a rapid and radical transformation of how we do things.

While several years ago Marxism would be listed as a major intellectual trend, it would appear that its revolutionary influence has passed. Some redefinition will be necessary if Marxism, or even revolutionary socialism, is to continue to play a role similar to that in the earlier decades of this century. Two widely known principles, however, continue to influence Europe, the United States, and many other areas throughout the world. Both existentialism and ecumenical Christianity attempt to offer any human being willing to listen the answer to an age old question, simply put, "what's it all about." For you and I it is an attempt to explain why we are alive on this planet, and at this time and place. These ideas are sometimes viewed as complex intellectual programs. Understanding them, and their interaction in today's world, gives the educated person a broad perspective on the world he or she lives in.

Chapter ◆ 31

Now we can see a new postwar Europe is taking shape. So long constrained by the emergence of the superpowers after World War II, the major European states embarked upon considerable social and economic reform which have transformed their societies. With the end of the Cold War, the European states will individually, and quite possibly in a collective manner, again play a major role in world affairs. Interestingly as the fiftieth anniversary of World War II events pass into history Germany is emerging again as a key player in Europe's future.

Germany since World War II has risen from the ashes. Heavily bombed, hated nearly world-wide, destitute, and occupied by foreign troops, the Federal Republic of Germany is today an example of modern industrial success. Enlightened, democratic leaders coupled with an industrious, creative, and hardworking population have ushered in an unprecedented era of prosperity for the German people. Since 1982 Chancellor Helmut Kohl fostered the economic success of his fellow West Germans. He welcomed, actively campaigned for, and engineered the reunification of the "Germanies." As a result, what seemed an improbability as the 1980's dawned has become a reality—a unified Germany. As noted above, the role of the new Germany may not be apparent for some time; but the early recognition of Croatia may be an indication of future German direction. Undoubtedly Germany will play an important role in the continuing process of European integration.

Often reluctant, the European states are moving toward a more formal integration by 1996. The European Economic Community, which has been at the center of these developments, is already redefining its position with the United States, the former Soviet Union, and nations throughout the world. Particularly, with a united Germany it appears that the postwar era of European subservience to the superpowers is over.

Former Soviet leader Mikhail Gorbachev has been responsible for a broad economic and political reform program not seen in Russia since Lenin's time. In the mid-1980s he played an impressive role on the world stage. Recognizing that despite vast military power the Soviet Union was falling behind in important economic areas, he advocated *"Perestroika,"* or restructuring in both a political and economic context. Equally unprecedented in this hitherto closed society has been the new openness or *"Glasnost,"* which has accompanied the vast changes taking place today. The Soviet Union's future is unclear, but it appears that ethnic inspired turmoil could alter the course of events there. Current President Boris Yeltsin is reaping the whirlwind created by his predecessor, once affectionately known as "Gorby."

The Soviet Union, now the Commonwealth of Independent States, has given up its dominance over Eastern Europe. Democratic principles and a yearning for what in the West are considered basic human liberties erupted there in largely, non-violent (the exception being Romania) pro-democracy movements throughout the latter part of 1989. Inspired by Poland's Solidarity movement of the early 1980s and in a different way by the government ordered massacre of demonstrators in Beijing, China's Tiananmen Square in June 1989, the former satellite states throughout Eastern Europe have begun to chart new courses for their respective economic and political systems.

We end the textbook, this study guide, and the course without a clear prediction of what might be ahead of us. Perhaps that is as it should be. For the study of history, in this case a survey of Western Civilization, is itself a constant reminder of how human beings similar to you and I have coped with their respective worlds. If history teaches us anything, it is that change is a part of life. All of the forerunners of our civilization today; Near Eastern, Greco-Roman, Medieval all endured change, and just as we are, were fashioned by it. As we look forward to the next century bear in mind all that has gone before us, all you have studied, and do so with the realization that we cannot be separated from our past—the Western heritage.

IDENTIFICATIONS

Identify each one of the following as used in the text. Refer to the text as necessary.

	Text Page
"Americanization of Europe"	738
decolonization	740-741
Second Agricultural Revolution	741-742
National Health Service	742
Soren Kierkegaard	744
Martin Heidegger	745
"the primacy of reason"	745
German Green Movement	747
Arab oil embargo	747
Chernobyl	747
The Second Sex	747
Karl Barth	748
The Screwtape Letters	749
Twenty-First Ecumenical Council	749
Pope John Paul II	749
Mikhail S. Gorbachev	749-751
Civic Forum	754-755
Nicolae Ceausescu	755
Boris Yeltsin	755-757
Commonwealth of Independent States (C.I.S.)	755-758
Slobodan Milosevic	760
St. Mary's Roman Catholic Church in Sarajevo	761

MAP EXERCISE A

On this map of the former Yugoslavia, mark the major geographic features, major cities, and the largest ethnic (states) subdivisions within this most unsettled land.

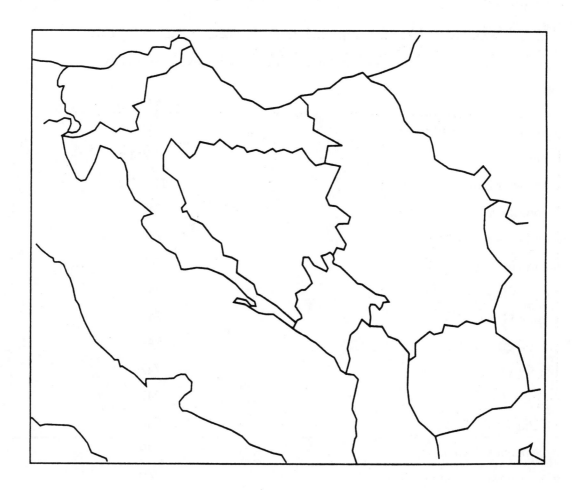

MAP EXERCISE B

This is our last map. Throughout this volume we have emphasized European areas. Given the global context of the world we live in today, it is fitting that we end with a map of the Pacific Rim.

On the accompanying map mark the location of all the states of North/South America and Asia that make up the Pacific Rim as we know it today.

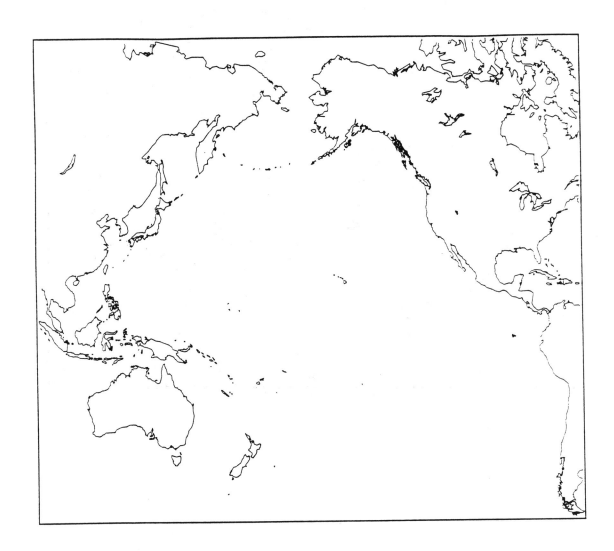

SHORT-ANSWER EXERCISE

Multiple-Choice

_____ 1.   The defining characteristics of European life as the Twentieth century ends appear to be: (a) environmentalism and consumerism, (b) environmentalism and Americanization, (c) Americanization and consumerism, (d) existentialism and socialism.

_____ 2.   Which is the most correct statement about modern women: (a) single women are replacing married women in the work force, (b) women are bearing children at an earlier age, (c) financial need and personal fulfillment are factors that encourage women to enter the work force, (d) none of these apply.

_____ 3.   (a) Human beings in extreme situations, (b) Fear and anxiety, (c) Death and dying, (d) All of these, are themes pursued by existential writers.

_____ 4.   Which of the following would not be found listed as a liberal theologian of this century: (a) C. S. Lewis, (b) Karl Barth, (c) Bishop John Robinson, (d) Paul Tillich.

_____ 5.   The pope most responsible for convening the Roman Church council known as Vatican II was: (a) Paul VI, (b) Pius X, (c) John Paul I, (d) John XXIII.

_____ 6.   The correct chronological order for the reign of the last four Popes would be: (a) John XXIII, John Paul I, Paul VI, John Paul II, (b) Paul VI, Pius X, John XXIII, John Paul II, (c) John XXIII, Paul VI, John Paul I, John Paul II, (d) John Paul I, John Paul II, Paul VI, John XXIII.

_____ 7.   The man most responsible for the collapse of the Soviet Empire was: (a) Mikhail S. Gorbachev, (b) Leonid Brezhnev, (c) Boris Yeltsin, (d) Constantin Chernenko.

_____ 8.   With the 1989 renunciation of the Brezhnev Doctrine the people of Eastern Europe: (a) moved to eliminate Soviet political dominance in their own states, (b) urged the suppression of Chinese student rioters in Beijing's Tiananmen Square, (c) demanded central planning of their national economies, (d) all of these are correct.

_____ 9.   Led by Czech playwright Václav Havel Civic Forum negotiated a series of reforms there which included each of the following except: (a) bringing non-communists into the government, (b) relaxation of censorship, (c) continuation of Marxist education, (d) elimination of travel restrictions on citizens.

_____ 10.   The authors conclude: (a) the continued use of reason, (b) continuous change, (c) environmental watchdogging, (d) ongoing material progress, represents the best hope for the future of the human race.

True-False

_____ 1. Clearly, the largest population expansion in European history took place between World War I and World War II.

_____ 2. The likelihood of a longer life has changed the relative position of child-bearing within a women's lifespan.

_____ 3. The so-called "student experience" before the Second World War was really only enjoyed by the privileged few.

_____ 4. Objectivity and the communal experience are standard themes of rock music.

_____ 5. Throughout the 1940s European clergymen stood silent against both Hitler's Nazism and the spread of communism.

_____ 6. The so-called "Brezhnev Doctrine" issued in 1968 called for peaceful coexistence with the United States.

_____ 7. After World War II Yugoslavia was the only communist country in Eastern Europe to pursue a course independent of Soviet domination.

_____ 8. I really have enjoyed all the work that this _Guidebook_ entailed.

_____ 9. Serbia's policies of "ethnic cleansing" have become urgent reminders of the horrors associated with World War II.

_____ 10. According to the text the spirit of criticism continues as a vital force in Western life.

Completion

1. For the first time in European history _____ has been available in large quantities.

2. _____ was the dominant philosophy of Europe at the mid-century mark.

3. Earlier thinkers such as _____ and _____ are considered fore-runners of modern existentialist thought.

4. The liberal theologian _____ argued that knowledge of the divine spirit had to be found through an examination of human nature and culture.

5. Pope John Paul II generally has reasserted the Catholic Church's traditional positions with regard to _____ and _____.

6. _____ is the term best used to express the vast political and economic changes currently underway in the Soviet Union.

7. The honorary re-burial of former Premier _____ was symbolic of the changes sweeping Hungary in the late 1980s

8. The so-called "velvet revolution" occurred in _____.

9. With regard to the current developments in _____ the authors state that no reliable predictions can be made.

10. Formed in 1955, and now in disarray, the _____ was designed to counter the U.S.-European alliance known as NATO.

FOR FURTHER CONSIDERATION

1. How do you assess the changing role of women in our time? Compare and contrast the advantages for society in this expanded participation, with what you see as disadvantages. Explain your position fully.

2. What does the textbook mean by the phrase, "the student experience"? How do you relate to that experience? Compare and contrast your own student experiences with those of the 1960s.

3. How would you characterize the current impact and future direction of the Christian heritage in our time?

4. In your opinion what will be the long-term effects of *perestroika* and *glasnost* on the Soviet Union? Do you see any potential disadvantages in this reform movement?

5. Keeping this last chapter in mind, as well as what you have learned throughout the course, how do you assess the future prospects of Western civilization. Explain your answer in depth.

Answers

Multiple-Choice

		Text Page
1.	C	738
2.	C	743
3.	D	745
4.	B	748
5.	D	749
6.	C	749
7.	A	749-750
8.	A	*passim*
9.	C	754
10.	A	761

True-False

1.	F	739
2.	T	743
3.	T	745
4.	F	746
5.	F	748
6.	F	751
7.	T	758
8.	T	*passim*
9.	T	760
10.	T	762

Completion

1.	food	738
2.	Existentialism	744
3.	Kierkegaard and Nietzsche	744
4.	Paul Tillich	748
5.	priesthood and the family (contraception)	749
6.	*perestroika*	750
7.	Imre Nagy	753
8.	Czechoslovakia (now the Czech Republic)	754
9.	Russia	757
10.	Warsaw Pact	761